⟁ W9-CAT-569

From Fear to Faith

Man's religious quest began with fear of the unknown, which he tried to control through magic, totem, taboo. But as his knowledge increased, so did his religious maturity. Fear became faith, a faith that life has meaning and purpose.

According to the author of this inspiring book, it is this faith that is the beginning and essence of all religions. From the Jainist to the Christian, the Moslem to the Taoist, the true believer affirms a reverence for life and a charity toward all men. However the great religions differ in outward form, these principles are characteristic of them all.

Mr. Gaer explains the philosophic tenets of these creeds with selections from their legends and writings—the sayings of Zarathustra, the lyrics of Lao-tze, Christ's Sermon on the Mount. Here is the magnificent spectrum of man's spiritual adventure—a lucid and revealing explanation of the eleven great religions of the world.

Included are an index, a bibliography, and a statistical table which enumerates the followers of the various religions today.

SIGNET and MENTOR Books
of Special Interest

☐ **HOW THE GREAT RELIGIONS BEGAN (revised) by Joseph Gaer.** A readable guide to man's quest for the spiritual, told through the inspiring lives of the world's religious leaders. (#Q4739—95¢)

☐ **RELIGION WITHOUT REVELATION by Julian Huxley.** The eminent scientist and philosopher lucidly explains the religion of humanism, its meaning, and aims. (#MQ984—95¢)

☐ **THE SERMON ON THE MOUNT According to Vedanta by Swami Prabhavananda.** A fascinating and superbly enlightening Hindu reading of the central gospel of Christianity by the renowned author of books on Indian religious philosophy. (#MY1150—$1.25)

☐ **HOW TO KNOW GOD: THE YOGA APHORISMS OF PATANJALI translated with Commentary by Swami Prabhavananda and Christopher Isherwood.** This classic work on yoga, its goal and methods, is essential to an understanding of Hindu religious practice. For more than fifteen hundred years the writings of Patanjali have been a principal influence on Hindu spiritual exercises. Index. (#MQ1230—95¢)

THE NEW AMERICAN LIBRARY, INC.,
P.O. Box 999, Bergenfield, New Jersey 07621

Please send me the SIGNET and MENTOR BOOKS I have checked above. I am enclosing $_____(check or money order—no currency or C.O.D.'s). Please include the list price plus 25¢ a copy to cover handling and mailing costs. (Prices and numbers are subject to change without notice.)

Name_____

Address_____

City_____State_____Zip Code_____
Allow at least 3 weeks for delivery

WHAT THE
Great Religions
Believe

by JOSEPH GAER

A SIGNET BOOK from
NEW AMERICAN LIBRARY
TIMES MIRROR

COPYRIGHT © 1963 BY JOSEPH GAER

*All rights reserved. No part of this book may be reproduced
in any form without permission in writing from the publisher.
For information address Dodd, Mead & Company,
79 Madison Avenue, New York, New York 10016.*

*This is an authorized reprint of a hardcover edition
published by Dodd, Mead & Company.*

SIGNET TRADEMARK REG. U.S. PAT. OFF. AND FOREIGN COUNTRIES
REGISTERED TRADEMARK—MARCA REGISTRADA
HECHO EN CHICAGO, U.S.A.

SIGNET, SIGNET CLASSICS, MENTOR, PLUME AND MERIDIAN BOOKS
*are published by The New American Library, Inc.,
1301 Avenue of the Americas, New York, New York 10019*

8 9 10 11 12 13 14 15 16

PRINTED IN THE UNITED STATES OF AMERICA

I do not know whether this book should be dedicated

To
FAY

or she should dedicate it to me—since we worked on it
together from A to Z

Preface

In the world today there are approximately three billion people, who belong to eleven major religions, which in turn are divided into a great number of sects and denominations. The religions vary in number of adherents, from Christianity, with over nine hundred million followers, to Zoroastrianism, whose followers account for less than a hundred and fifty thousand and are decreasing.

In each religion and denomination there are adherents of various degrees of involvement and religious feeling, as well as with various degrees of clarity about their beliefs. Nearly all people belong to the religion and denomination into which they were born, and accept it naturally, and are loyal to it in much the same way as they are loyal to their nationality. They conform to the church into which they are born and follow the rituals without questioning them or without always knowing the beliefs behind them. And most are comfortable in their belonging, which satisfies their communal need and identification. Among the vast numbers of the laity, if all of them do not know the basic beliefs that gave rise to the rituals and traditions of their own religion and denomination, they understandably know less about the beliefs of other religions.

In this book the attempt is made to present, briefly and without entering into sectarianism, the basic beliefs of the religions followed in the world today.

Contents

10. ISLAM: *Submission to Allah*

11. ZOROASTRIANISM: *The Refugee Religion*

12. ZEN BUDDHISM: *Riddles with a Purpose*

1 WHAT IS RELIGION?

The Search

1. Stop Right Here

Consider for one long moment the title of this book: what each word in it means, and what jointly they propose to explore.

"What"

This merely indicates that this book is an elaborate answer to a question. Essentially, this is true of every lecture, play, film or book. For each implies a question and attempts to give an answer. The question may be trite and the answer obvious; the question may be superficial, and the answer stereotyped; or the question may be profound, and the answer evasive. It also may take any of the many other forms of questions-and-answers.

"The Great Religions"

The great religions are the living religions. Not that religions really ever die. If the culture in which they were born and thrived changes radically, and the faith no longer plays an important role in the acts and judgments of the living generations, the religions become transformed and adapt to their environment. Sometimes gradually and sometimes violently, the parent religion is supplanted and new generations align themselves with what they consider an entirely new religion. Yet, in fact, upon scrutiny the new religions are found to retain much of the old in new garb. The living religions are those that have a following in the present, though each one may be splintered into hundreds of sects and denominations, which concern themselves with modes of devotion and ritual. Our objective will be briefly to present the major faiths in the world today.

"Believe."

The major beliefs of each religion will be given against the origins or founders of each organized faith, without deviating into sectarian interpretations.

There remains the word "religion" to be defined. What do we understand by the word "religion"?

This is a question much easier asked than answered.

Many writers on comparative religion show a distinct reluctance to give a definition. Readers are cautioned at the outset in Edward Norbeck's excellent book, *Religion in Primitive Society:* "Authors of books on religion which attempt to be comparative in scope or to deal with religion in a general sense, are usually quick to state that religion is difficult to define." That it is. But such observations do not help us any. Another writer, Frederick Spiegelberg, in *Living Religions of the World,* goes even further: "It may sound as though I were about to propose a definition of religion. I am not. To do so would be a fatal error; for religion is utterly indefinable."

Such examples can be multiplied. While writers are understandably hesitant to commit themselves to a definition either because it is difficult to define or because the attempt to do so may prove "a fatal error," if we are to inquire into what the living religions believe, we must first know what "religion" *is,* or the entire inquiry would be "a fatal error."

The following is an attempt, a rather lengthy attempt, to define religion and to indicate its place in man's experience of reality.

To begin with, religion is very old.

As far as we can determine, religion has existed in every society, from the most primitive to the most culturally advanced. The more keys modern science finds with which to open the locked doors of the past, and the more we learn about the early days of man on earth, the more evidence there is that all these societies in the past had one thing in common—some form of religion.

Until about a century or two ago it was generally believed that human history began not very long before recorded history, which is estimated around seven or, at most, eight thousand years. But anthropology, the science of man-come-lately, has unearthed proof that many thousands of years ago there already roamed upon the earth an advanced type of human being, straight and tall, with a high forehead and a large brain, and with a comparatively advanced culture in tools made of flint and bone, jewelry produced from shells and ivory, as well as remarkable multi-colored paintings.

Some of these early men were more advanced than others. And while some progressed continually in an upward trend, others remained stationary after reaching a certain stage of development. Still others retrogressed. Yet all of these early men, whatever their rate of development or whatever their differences, left behind unmistakable signs that they had each practiced a religion of their own.

Within the last century discoveries throughout the world

have begun to reveal the range of human beings, which anthropologists classify as "Java Man," "Neanderthal Man," "Cro-Magnon," "Galley Hill," and so on.

These human beings apparently belonged to different races, having a diversity of characteristics, or an intermingling of certain features. They had different languages and different cultures. These peoples obviously migrated great distances, and populated various parts of the earth ever so long ago— about four or five hundred thousand years ago or more. And all these early peoples had one feature in common—each of them practiced a religion.

A very long time must have passed before man evolved to this state as a member of Homo sapiens—upright walking, with a large brain, capable of communicating within his group through language, and roaming the earth to conquer his environment.

The first demand made upon his brain (which in turn stimulated its development) was to subdue his environment —to keep warm when and where it was cold; to keep cool when and where it was hot; to find an abundant supply of food where food was scarce; to domesticate animals and, later, much later, to add assurance to his food supply by growing grain. He developed hunting devices; he made use of his discovery of fire.

Many theories have been presented on how man first discovered a way to start a fire, to keep it going, and to put it out or control it. Whichever theory may be the correct one, this discovery advanced man far along on his road to civilization.

Two aptitudes peculiar to man enabled him to develop and progress rapidly: He could speak, and he could conceive of a "tomorrow."

However limited and faulty his speech was (and to a certain extent still is), he was able to communicate. That gave him the advantage of sharing and preserving his experiences with other members of his group. For thousands and tens of thousands of years before man invented writing he preserved his experiences through telling them to others— through oral teachings. In time a class of people developed who were especially gifted in the art of oral teaching and who knew how to impress upon the younger generation whatever the elders wanted them to remember in meeting the hazards and particular problems that might confront them in the future.

His awareness of a tomorrow made it possible for early man to worry about and to plan his future security.

With these two faculties as aids and guides, he set himself (collectively) to prepare in advance for whatever he thought he needed for his security on the morrow—his shelter, his safety, his food, his well-being. These involved a variety of ever-increasing activities. And in doing all these things he established himself as master of his often hostile environment.

2. Four Ways to Experience Reality

a. *Knowing*

In the process of overcoming the dangers of his environment, early man acquired a vast amount of knowledge about the world in which he lived. He did not acquire this knowledge deliberately, nor was his knowledge gained or organized in an orderly fashion. It accrued from his acute need to know. His senses, sharpened by fear of dangers seen and many more dangers imagined, helped him to preserve his experiences and later organize them in his storehouse-memory.

Early man knew the world about him, as we today know it, through his senses. Man's senses are not perfect, or even very good, as we now know. But whatever man felt he most needed for his existence or survival, that he observed with scrupulous attention. And in time he accumulated a remarkable amount of knowledge about a great number of things. He preserved this accumulation of knowledge through oral teachings and folklore.

He observed the plants and all growing things, some good to the eye and taste, and pleasant to smell. And he learned to distinguish between fruits and plants that he could safely eat and those injurious to him.

He observed the living things about him everywhere: the animals on dry land, the birds in the air, and the many varieties of fish in the waters of the lakes and seas. He early learned which he could eat and which to avoid.

He observed the changes in the weather and the changes of the seasons. And he noticed that all things changed with the passing of time.

He became aware of Time.

He observed the day as a recurrent measure of time. He divided the day into four parts: morning, afternoon, evening and night. He could not (and we still cannot) decide whether the day begins in the morning, at noon, at sunset or at midnight. (For most people in the world the day begins at midnight; for others the day begins at sunset; for mariners the day begins at noon when the sun is at its zenith.) But the day, regardless of when it began, was the measure.

He observed the rotation of the moon around the earth in almost (but not quite) twenty-eight days, which he called a moon-month. And he divided the month into equal parts, calling each part a "week."

Man had difficulty determining the length of the week. Ancient Egyptians observed a ten-day week. Early Romans observed an eight-day week. But long before that a seven-day week had been adopted. And each day was believed to be ruled over by one of the seven celestial bodies: the sun, the moon, and the then-known planets—Mars, Mercury, Jupiter, Venus and Saturn. This belief was later reflected in the names given to the days: Sun-day (Sunday); Moon-day (Monday); Mars-day (Tuesday); Mercury-day (Wednesday); Jupiter-day (Thursday); Venus-day (Friday); and Saturn-day (Saturday). (Each group of course had different words for the names of the planets. The English names come from the Anglo-Saxon: Sunnan-day, Monan-day, Tiwes-day, Wodnes-day, Thunres-day, Frige-day and Saeter-day.)

Man also observed the rotation of the solar year, which divided naturally into four seasons: spring, summer, autumn and winter. But many things about time puzzled him. He could not, for instance, find any solution to the problem of dividing the natural, or solar, year by the lunar month. And that continued to trouble him for a long time.

Very early, man became aware of the heavenly bodies and sought, and thought he could obtain, answers from the stars to many of the questions that plagued him. He spent much time observing the celestial bodies, for he believed that they influenced all the events in his life.

He became aware of Space.

He noticed that the winds came, and with them they brought a change of weather. He also noticed that where the wind came from made the difference. And that set him thinking about how far in any direction one might go before the end of space would be reached.

He saw the earth as a huge, uneven disc, covered with mountains and valleys, surrounded by large bodies of water. The heavens above he saw as a vaulted space in which the sun, the moon and the stars were suspended. And from his observation of the heavenly bodies he had learned of their motions. He concluded that the sun, the moon, and all the stars rotated around the earth.

He had not, nor could he have had, any idea of the age or vastness of the universe. However observant, from examining the heavens with the naked eye he could not conclude that the sun was 300,000 times more massive than the earth, and that it was nearly 400 times further away than the moon. He had no way of estimating weights and distances in space.

Although his observations were often faulty, man learned much, and he learned quickly. His very survival depended upon a meticulous scrutiny of his surroundings. And this fear-sharpened observation, in time, resulted in developing his many skills and his rudimentary knowledge. From his observations of the behavior of the smallest insects, to the movements of the heavenly bodies, he slowly gathered what was later organized and became departmentalized sciences —from astronomy to zoology.

b. *Understanding*

Man tried to understand the principles underlying and governing the world around him. He began to ask why things behaved as they did. He began to seek the reasons for a myriad of phenomena he had observed. And while his senses helped him in his observations, the reasons he sought could neither be seen nor touched, neither heard nor smelt. They were beyond the senses.

He tried from the start to correlate essential experiences and draw conclusions about them or from them. He tried to understand them. His senses made him aware of the world outside himself, but he attempted to fathom its nature and behavior. He tried to reason out why things are as they are and why they behave as they behave. Everything seemed to be governed by fixed laws. Though he could not clearly comprehend them, he tried to find out the principles governing things in nature.

Later—much, much later—this attempt to understand or reason out the principles or laws governing everything in nature was called the search for wisdom, or the law of wisdom, which in Greek is called Philosophy.

The need to *understand* as well as to *know* developed very early, and primitive man has now been given credit for his perception, as well as his vast and varied accumulation of knowledge.

When primitive man began to grapple with the principles behind reality (however faultily from our point of view) he was able to increase his knowledge and bring order into his growing societal life.

Every living creature, from a flea to an elephant, possesses within itself the means of adapting to survive in a given environment. Sometimes the natural environment changes radically, and those living things perish which cannot adapt themselves to meet the changed conditions. But man, because of his superior adaptive organ, his brain, managed to survive catastrophic changes in climate, floods, scarcity of food, and ravaging disease. And he could even anticipate and prepare for certain changes.

c. *Believing*

While his understanding of the world grew, and to some extent satisfied man's quest to know the "what" and "why" of things, certain puzzling questions gnawed at him and gave him no peace from the very start:

What had created the world, and when?

To whom did the earth belong and for whom was it created?

Why were there so many various living things on earth? And who had dominion over them?

He could not find the answers to these questions through his observation; nor could he arrive at them through reason. He could only believe there must be a purpose to man's life, and to life in general. Though he still did not know what that purpose was, he concluded, from observing order in nature, that it must exist.

From this belief, that life had purpose in general, in which the individual was involved, arose the institution of religion. The word itself, it is believed, comes from the Latin "religere," which means "to be involved."

d. *Creating*

There is still another area in the experience of reality in addition to *knowing*, *understanding* and *believing*, which also goes back to the beginning of societal life and is part of every known culture.

This experience took many ever-evolving forms:

It was expressed in sounds, both joyful and sorrowful, to convey a great variety of moods.

It took shape in clay and stone images.

It was communicated in sand-paintings and in the use of the many multi-colored objects and materials available to man around his dwelling place.

It was conveyed through the movements of the body in dance.

It reached amazing power through rhythmic patterns in language that were used to express concepts and emotions.

These were the *arts*. And the arts were related to religion.

Primitive man (as, indeed, most men living today) could not meditate on abstractions very long. He (and we) clothed ideas in concrete symbols and surrounded them by rituals. The more abstract the concept, the more concrete became the ritual and ceremony encircling the idea. In time the concept or idea evolved and changed, although the ritual remained and continued to be observed. Often man accepted the ritual as traditionally practiced and called it his religion.

As man's knowledge and understanding grew, his faith, too, went through a cycle of changes.

There still exist, or existed until very recently, remnants of primitive or aboriginal people who had spread from pole to pole. Anthropologists studied them and recorded their great diversity of features, skills, languages, and, above all, their cultures. Special study was given to that part of their culture which evidenced concepts of the supernatural, or religious moral teachings, or fixed rituals and ceremonies. However different these primitive people, and however varied their practices and taboos, they each had a defined religion.

In primitive societies religion was made concrete through a variety of images, which represented forces in nature. And each image was venerated for the specific blessings it presumably could bestow, or feared for the punishment it could inflict upon those who turned away from the behavior prescribed by the elders and the priesthood.

Early man did not, nor could he, have a clear idea of his place in the universe; though his mythology testifies that he often speculated about it. He observed the heavens, in which appeared the sun, the moon, and the stars. He saw the earth, which seemed stationary, with sun and moon and stars revolving around it. He could see the trees bearing fruit, the great and small fish in the lakes and seas, and the wide variety of animals in the forest which he hunted for food. And he came to believe that all he saw about him had been created for his particular benefit. He had, as modern scientists would describe it, an anthropocentric concept of the world— the concept that man was the center of the world, and it was for him that everything had been created.

Yet his dominant feeling was not self-confidence, but fear. And his persistent search was for purpose in the crude cosmogony he was able to construct.

Fear played a prominent role in the development and growth of the religions of all mankind. First came the fear of the unpredictable forces of nature—earthquakes, floods, drought and hurricanes. Then came the fear of illness, pestilence and the tribulations that afflict the aged. The strongest fear of all was the fear of death. Man could not accept death and total extinction.

Yet there is a danger in accepting fear as the exclusive emotion responsible for the institution of religion. Fear—fear of the unknown or the unpredictable and, above all, the fear of death had, and has, its part in the architecture of religion. But the dominant part in man's creation and development of religion is the belief that life has purpose.

Man could not confirm it by his senses. He could not prove it by his reason. He could only assume it by faith.

And that belief that life has purpose is the beginning and essence of religion.

To live in accord with this belief, men everywhere have established codes of behavior (and clothed them in appropriate rituals and ceremonies) which differ from one another in practice, though they are often similar in theory, particularly at their starting point. And commandments were formulated to keep the believers in harmony with and dedicated to, their basic concepts of life's purpose.

In this book we shall examine the basic beliefs of the great religions, which evolved from a common source—the search for the purpose of life.

2 HINDUISM

"A Fellowship of Faiths"

1. The Age of the World

In Hindu societies—among those who follow Hinduism, Buddhism, and Jainism—it is believed that Man appeared on the world scene at an inconceivably remote point of time. The Hindus consider the world as part of a beginningless and endless process which follows fixed cycles known as "Days of Brahma." Each Day of Brahma lasts about four and a half billion years. Adherents of Jainism, an ascetic offshoot of Hinduism, believe that their founder (the first of twenty-four) appeared one hundred trillion (100,000 million) *palyas* ago. And if one should ask what period of time is represented by a *palya*, the answer would be that a *palya* is the length of time that it would take to empty a well one mile square and one mile deep, full of fine hair, if one hair is taken out every hundred years. This is their allegorical way of saying that they believe the world always existed and always will exist.

This view is a basic difference between the Judaeo-Christian-Islamic religions and the Hindu religions. The first three believe the entire universe was created about six thousand years ago; and the latter believe that the world has always existed though in a constant, if gradual, state of transformation. In what they refer to as "the Night of Brahma," the world is in a state of chaos and dissolution; and in "the Day of Brahma" it is being re-formed or re-created. And one day and night of Brahma lasts about four and a half billion years.

Another basic difference between the Judaeo-Christian-Islamic and the Hindu beliefs concerns the universe. The first group believe that the world was created, and someday in the unknown future it will end. The Hindus believe that the world always was and always will be. It will change, but it will never end.

The historic period of man, as we now know, is minute as compared with the prehistoric period; for while the historic period is measured in centuries (and they are as yet few), the prehistoric period is measured in millennia (and they are very many).

All human institutions of the comparatively brief historic period are deeply rooted in the incalculably long prehistoric period. All we know and believe has its origin in primitive myths and mythmaking, in animism and polytheism, in idolatry and fetishism, and in every conceivable— what we now call—superstition. But we should always remember that the superstitions were part of the religions, and were no less sacred to the people who believed them than our beliefs and creeds to us. Max Müller, the great nineteenth-century German orientalist and translator of *The Sacred Books of the East,* once wrote: "There never was a false god, nor was there really ever a false religion, unless you call a child a false man."

2. The Hindu Triad

India has been the stage of intense religious activity for a number of millennia. And the religion of India, Hinduism, has shown an extraordinary tolerance to other faiths which have been brought into the country. It therefore absorbed influences from without as well as evolved from within. And it passed through a number of stages, or periods, which are reflected in the sacred books. Some Hindu scholars regard Hinduism as "a fellowship of Faiths."

Hinduism has no founder; and it has no fixed creed. But it does have a number of beliefs which are held by most, if not all, Hindus. The central belief of Hinduism is that there is one Universal Spirit, or Eternal Essence, without beginning or end, called *Brahman;* which means, the World-Soul. This World-Soul is the Three-in-One God, called the *Trimutri.* He is called the Three-in-One God because they believe *Brahman* is:

Brahma, the Creator;
Vishnu, the Preserver; and
Shiva, the Destroyer.

These are not separate one from the other—even though they are different—but are different aspects or manifestations of the same divine Unity. In addition to *Brahma, Vishnu* and *Shiva,* there are a great many other attributes of the Triad which have been symbolized, and are called gods. But in Hinduism, the word "god" does not carry the same meaning as it does in other religions. And they do not claim that *Brahman* loves or hates, compensates or punishes, or has any other anthropomorphic characteristics.

Hindus believe that the Triad which evolved from the World-Soul are continually creating and evolving and changing the world. At the end of a cycle, called a "Day of Brahma," Shiva destroys the old world, Brahma creates a new one, and Vishnu appears on earth in different human forms, or incarnations, to preserve the world and to guide and enlighten man.

3. The Soul's Garment

Man is considered as not outside the World-Soul but as part of it. Man consists of body and soul. The body is like an outer robe that one puts away when outworn. The soul endures forever. The body is ruled by passion and desires and meaningless ambitions. But the soul is ruled by serenity and the tranquil search for truth.

"The wise in heart mourn not for those who live, nor for those who die." So begins the second chapter of the *Bhagavad-Gita* (The Lord's Song) of the great Hindu epic called the *Mahabharata.* The wise in heart try to live their temporal lives not controlled by their physical desires or swayed by the deception of their senses, but in calm harmony with their soul, which is birthless and deathless.

One must not be moved by either joy or sorrow, but submit to fate, if one wishes to attain truth and understand the ultimate nature of reality. The wise in heart are cautioned to scorn those who follow virtue for its reward. Doing the right thing is its own reward. If any other rewards are expected, the acts are no longer right. And each right act must be preceded by right thinking; the right thinking must be preceded by tranquillity. And tranquillity, according to the *Bhagavad-Gita,* "comes to him who deals with objects of the senses not loving and not hating, making them serve his free soul, which remains serenely lord."

4. Where the Castes Came From

Hinduism is the only religion that believes in a caste system. Brahma, so Hinduism teaches, created the first man, named Manu. Out of Manu's head came the best and holiest people. They were called *Brahmins.* Out of Manu's hands came the rulers and warriors. They were called *Kshatriyas.* Out of Manu's thighs came the craftsmen of the world, called *Vaisyas.* And out of Manu's feet came the rest of the people, called *Sudras.* Thus Brahma the Creator determined that there should be four different castes of people.

The *Brahmins,* who belong to the highest caste, are the priests and philosophers, dedicated to the study of the sacred books, and they are supported by the State or the other castes. *Brahmins* are vegetarians, bathe twice daily in flowing water, and wear the sacred thread that is a symbol of their status. All other castes must do honor to them and even the royal or ruling family must show them the greatest respect.

Those who belong to the *Kshatriyas* engage in all manner of governmental and legal activities and professions. They have prescribed religious duties to perform, but owe respect to the *Brahmins.* This caste represents the upper middle class of Indian society.

The *Vaisyas* minister to the material needs of their fellow countrymen. They are the merchants, farmers and industrialists. While they are below the *Brahmins* and the *Kshatriyas,* they are above the rest of the population in distinction and religious privileges.

The duty or fate of the *Sudras* is to serve the rest of the people as workmen, artisans, farm laborers, servants and gardeners. They are not permitted to study the *Vedas* (the sacred books of Hinduism) and are excluded from many religious duties, or participation in rituals.

In time the caste system became divided and subdivided into many other castes within each caste, until there were thousands of castes in India. And no member of a lower caste could rise to a position within one considered higher, or even eat or drink with a member of a higher caste. He could not marry into a caste higher than his own, nor could he worship within the same temple, or be buried in the same burial ground.

Soon there appeared in India people who did not belong to even the lowest of the thousands of castes. They were pariahs and outcastes of their society. And they came to be known as "untouchables" because contact with them was supposed to pollute and degrade any caste members. Though no one knows precisely the origin of the Outcastes, it is believed that they were the offspring of intermarriages forbidden between the castes, or the children of illicit unions. This large casteless class serve as butchers and as gravediggers, and do other tasks considered degrading.

The Outcastes caused many uprisings in India during the early part of the twentieth century. Mahatma Gandhi was one of the leaders who devoted much of his time and energy toward restoring a caste status to these people. He also led a strong movement for the abolition of castes. But since the caste system is not only condoned but prescribed by the Laws of Manu, it continues to exist in the social order of the Hindus.

5. From Good Must Come Good

Hinduism believes in the Law of the Deed, called *Karma*. This law teaches: *From good must come good; and from evil, evil.*

Every thought and every act is either good or bad. Each is compensated or punished accordingly; if not immediately, then in a subsequent incarnation. What we think and what we do determine inexorably what we are or are going to be. This is *Karma*. What we are now is the result of our thoughts and deeds in past incarnations; and what we think or do in our lives will determine what we will be like in the next incarnation. Suicide is obviously no escape. One can kill the body but not the soul. The only solution is to think and act in a way that will eventually accrue enough merit to compensate in a future rebirth.

"The end of birth is death; and the end of death is birth:

this is ordained." So it is written in the *Bhagavad-Gita*. The body of man is like a garment. When it becomes outworn through age or illness, the soul leaves it and is reincarnated in the body of a new-born baby. So Hinduism believes.

The belief in a life hereafter is held by other religions. Even reincarnation, in the way it is interpreted in Hinduism, appears in other living religions. But reincarnation as a continuous process, combined with the Karmaic Law—so that as soon as an individual dies he is reborn, and either punished for all the evil he has done, or rewarded for all the good he has done—this is peculiar to the religion of Hinduism.

Mahatma Gandhi, in a letter to one of his disciples, wrote:

The more I observe and study things, the more convinced I become that sorrow over separation and death is perhaps the greatest delusion. To realize that it is a delusion is to become free. There is no death, no separation of the substance. And yet the tragedy of it is that though we love friends for the substance we recognize in them, we deplore the destruction of the insubstantial that covers the substance for the time being. Whereas real friendship should be used to reach the whole through the fragment. You seem to have got the truth for the moment. Let it abide for ever . . .

What you say about rebirth is sound. It is nature's kindness that we do not remember past births. Where is the good either of knowing in detail the numberless births we have gone through? Life would be a burden if we carried such a tremendous load of memories. A wise man deliberately forgets many things, even as a lawyer forgets the cases and their details as soon as they are disposed of. Yes, "death is but a sleep and a forgetting" . . .

Mother is slowly going. It will be well if the end comes soon. It is better to leave a body one has outgrown. To wish to see the dearest ones as long as possible in the flesh is a selfish desire and it comes out of weakness or want of faith in the survival of the soul after the dissolution of the body. The form ever changes, ever perishes, the informing spirit neither changes nor perishes. True love consists in transferring itself from the body to the dweller within and then necessarily realizing the oneness of all life inhabiting numberless bodies. . . . Both birth and death are great mysteries. If death is not a prelude to another life, the intermediate period is a cruel mockery.*

* *Reincarnation Anthology*, ed. Joseph Head and S. L. Cranston (New York: Julian Press, Inc.)

6. The King and Bhanto Nagasena

The difficult concept of reincarnation is presented in the following story-form, one of many used in Hindu literature to illustrate the beliefs of Hinduism:

The king said: "Bhanto Nagasena, does rebirth take place without anything transmigrating (passing over)?"

"Yes, Your Majesty. Rebirth takes place without anything transmigrating."

"How, Bhanto Nagasena, does rebirth take place without anything transmigrating? Give an illustration."

"Suppose, Your Majesty, a man were to light a light from another light; pray, would the one light have passed over (transmigrated) to the other light?"

"No, verily, Bhanto."

"In exactly the same way, Your Majesty, does rebirth take place without anything transmigrating."

"Give another illustration."

"Do you remember, Your Majesty, having learnt, when you were a boy, some verse or other from your professor of poetry?"

"Yes, Bhanto."

"Pray, Your Majesty, did the verse pass over (transmigrate) to you from your teacher?"

"No, verily, Bhanto."

"In exactly the same way, Your Majesty, does rebirth take place without anything transmigrating."

"Bhanto Nagasena," said the king, "what is it that is born into the next existence."

"Your Majesty," said the elder, "it is name and form that is born into the next existence."

7. The Yogas

If the soul of man is deathless and is reincarnated generation after generation, carrying forward compensation or punishment, according to the Karmaic Law, then what ultimate promise is there for the individual soul that has led the good life? What release awaits him from the burden of the cycle of reincarnation?

Hinduism believes that individual souls, which are like sparks of the Eternal Essence, when purified by good, are finally released from the bondage of reincarnation in the flesh. And the soul is joined with the World-Soul forever. This state is called *Nirvana*.

And it is the belief of Hinduism that as an aid in reaching *Nirvana*, there are certain disciplines, known as *Yogas*. These disciplines are of great antiquity, and are mentioned in the *Vedas* (the sacred books of this religion). The first discipline of *Yoga* is prolonged immobility and controlled breathing. The physical disciplines are necessary to gain complete concentration for the effort to identify with the Absolute—with the Brahman.

There are various kinds of *Yogas* and various stages of development in all of them. After complete physical control, comes control of the emotions, and moral purity, which makes possible total concentration.

There is also the Law of Moral Order (*Dharma*), according to Hinduism, which each individual must discover for himself. For each race, each caste, each family group has its *Dharma*. They are not the same. But they lead to the same ultimate objective: reunion with the World-Soul.

8. The Sacred Vedas

All Hindus have a deep reverence for the eldest of their sacred books, the *Vedas* (Books of Knowledge). The four Vedic books are vast collections of hymns to a number of gods; prayers that accompany sacrifices; chants to be sung to traditional melodies; spells and incantations; beliefs for the rich and beliefs for the poor; and devotional prayers.

The most ancient and best-known of the *Vedas* is the *Rig-Veda*, a collection of about 1200 hymns addressed to various nature gods, though chiefly to Indra, god of storms and winds, and Angi, god of fire.

One of these hymns is of particular interest, for it describes Creation, and affords comparison with the first chapter of Genesis in the Bible. This hymn from the *Rig-Veda* was translated by Ralph T. Griffith, who was president of Benares College in India over a century ago.

9. Creation Hymn

Then was not non-existent nor existent; there was no realm of air, no sky beyond it.

What covered in, and where and what gave shelter? Was water there, unfathomed depth of water?

Death was not then, nor was there aught immortal: no sign was there, the day's and night's divider.

That One Thing, breathless, breathed by its own nature; apart from it was nothing whatsoever.

Darkness there was: at first concealed in darkness this All was indiscriminated chaos.

All that existed then was void and formless: by the great power of Warmth was born that Unit.

Thereafter rose Desire in the beginning—Desire, the primal seed and germ of Spirit.

Sages who searched with their heart's thought discovered the existent's kinship in the non-existent.

Transversely was their severing line extended: what was above it then, and what below it?

There were begetters, there were mighty forces, free action here and energy up yonder.

Who verily knows and who can here declare it, whence it was born and whence comes this creation?

The Gods are later than this world's production. Who knows then whence it first came into being?

He, the first origin of this creation, whether he formed it all or did not form it,

Whose eye controls this world in highest heaven, he verily knows it, or perhaps he knows not.

To the *Vedas* have been added many tomes of commentaries, called *Upanishads,* which attempt to explain the ultimate nature of reality. The original *Vedas* and their numerous commentaries have produced a multitude of sects, each breaking off because of their disagreement on interpretations of some of the articles of faith or certain rituals followed in performing their devotion.

In the sixth century B.C., two great Hindu dissenters arose who, as we shall see later, became the founders of two religions, and challenged some of the teachings of the *Vedas.* But those who remained within the fold of Hinduism also adapted themselves to changing times, and reinterpreted their beliefs to correspond to new conditions of life. The *Vedas,* however, continue to exert a great influence on the Hindus. Many of the sacrifices, traditions and rituals were abandoned, displaced, or modified, but the essential beliefs as given in the *Vedas* continue to exert a strong hold on the followers of Hinduism.

The sacred books of Hinduism are more numerous than those of any other religion. In addition to the canonical works, such as the *Vedas,* the *Brahmanas* (commentaries on the *Vedas*) and the *Upanishads,* which are mystic speculations, there are a number of apocryphal works held in high esteem and which, today, are better known and exert a greater influence upon Hindus than the canonical works, known principally to theologians and scholars.

10. Two Great Epics

Two great and very long epics in particular have left their mark on the soul of every Hindu. One of these epics is the *Ramayana,* which means the Adventures of Rama. It tells the story of Vishnu the Preserver, who appeared in his seventh Incarnation as Prince Rama, son of King Dasaratha, ruler of the Children of the Sun. Rama's mission on earth was to save mankind from evil, represented by the Ruler of the Giants, King Ravan.

This epic is part of the Hindu Scriptures and has been kept fresh in the hearts of many generations of Hindus through an annual ten-day pageant. The pageant stresses the victories of Rama, who lived, according to tradition, a million and three hundred thousand years ago. Actually the ten-day holiday, called *Durga Puja,* is dedicated to the worship of the Divine Mother. But two hours of each of the *Durga Puja* are devoted to a dramatic reading of the *Ramayana;* this ends with the celebrants burning King Ravan in effigy.

More influential in Hinduism is the much longer epic, called *Mahabharata* (The Great Brothers). In this epic Vishnu, in his Incarnation as Krishna, expounds his doctrines in a section known as the *Bhagavad-Gita* (The Lord's Song). The perfect warrior in the epic, Arjuna, appeals to Krishna on the eve of a great battle. Arjuna is not certain he can distinguish the right from the wrong course of action. He pleads:

> How can I, in the battle, shoot with shafts
> On Bhishma, or on Drona—oh, thou Chief!
> Both worshipful, both honorable men?

> Better to live on beggar's bread
>   With those we love alive,
> Than taste their blood in rich feast spread,
>   And guiltily survive!
> Ah! were it worse—who knows?—to be
>   Victor or vanquished here,
> When those confront us angrily
>   Whose death leaves living drear?

In pity lost, by doubtings tossed,
   My thoughts—distracted—turn
To Thee, the Guide I reverence most,
   That I may counsel learn.

Krishna's long and involved answers to relieve Arjuna's
distress masterfully delineate the philosophical and theo-
logical principles of Hinduism:

You grieve where no grief should be! You speak
Words lacking wisdom! For the wise in heart
Mourn not for those that live, nor those that die.
Nor I, nor you, nor any one of these,
Ever was not, nor ever will not be,
Forever and forever afterwards.
All, that does live, lives always! To man's frame
As there come infancy and youth and age,
So come the raisings-up and layings-down
Of other and still other life-abodes,
Which the wise know, and fear not. This that irks—
Your sense-life, thrilling to the elements—
Bringing you heat and cold, sorrows and joys,
Is brief and mutable! Bear with it, Prince!
As the wise bear. The soul which is not moved,
The soul that with a strong and constant calm
Takes sorrow and takes joy indifferently,
Lives in the life undying! That which is
Can never cease to be; that which is not
Will not exist. To see this truth of both
Is theirs who part essence from accident,
Substance from shadow. Indestructible,
Learn! the Life is, spreading life through all;
It cannot anywhere, by any means,
Be anywise diminished, stayed or changed.
. . . End and Beginning are dreams!
Birthless and deathless and changeless remains the
   spirit forever;
Death has not touched it at all, dead though the
   house of it seems!

Know me, as I am, the very Truth.
Earth, water, flame, air, ether, life, and mind
And individuality—those eight
Make up the showing of me, Manifest.
. . . All these hang on me
As hangs a row of pearls upon its string.
I am the fresh taste of the water; I

The silver of the moon, the gold of the sun,
The word of worship in the Veda, the thrill
That passes in the ether, and the strength
Of man's shed seed. I am the good sweet smell
Of the moistened earth, I am the fire's red light.
The vital air moving in all which moves,
The holiness of hallowed souls, the root
Undying, whence has sprung whatever is;
The wisdom of the wise, the intellect
Of the informed, the greatness of the great,
The splendor of the splendid!

I am the Sacrifice! I am the Prayer!
I am the Funeral-Cake set for the dead!
I am the healing herb! I am the ghee,
The Mantra, and the flame, and that which burns!
I am—of all this boundless Universe—
The Father, Mother, Ancestor, and Guard!
The Way, the Fosterer, the Lord, the Judge,
The Witness; the Abode, the Refuge-House,
The Friend, the Fountain and the Sea of Life
Which sends, and swallows up; Treasure of Worlds
And Treasure-Chamber! Seed and Seed-Sower,
Whence endless harvests spring! Sun's heat is mine;
Heaven's rain is mine to grant or to withhold;
Death am I, and Immortal Life I am,
Arjuna! Sat and Asat, Visible Life,
And Life Invisible!

Then Arjuna asks:

Lord! Of the men who serve You—true in heart—
As God revealed; and of the men who serve
Worshiping You Unrevealed, Unbodied, far,
Which take the better way of faith and life?

And Krishna answers:

. . . Who hates nought
Of all which lives, living himself benign,
Compassionate, from arrogance exempt,
Exempt from love of self, unchangeable
By good or ill; patient, contented, firm
In faith, mastering himself, true to his word,
Seeking Me, heart and soul; vowed unto me—
That man I love!
. . . Who to the friend and foe

Keeping an equal heart, with equal mind
Bears shame and glory, with an equal peace
Takes heat and cold, pleasure and pain; abides
Quit of desires, hears praise or calumny
In passionless restraint, unmoved by each,
Linked by no ties to earth, steadfast to Me,
That man I love!

This great poetic work has won readers the world over. So sacred is the *Mahabharata* considered by the Hindus that they believe reading it "destroys all sin and creates virtue." And the statement is made at the very opening of the *Mahabharata*, that reciting a single stanza "is enough to wipe away much evil."

11. What Hinduism Believes

Just as the attributes of the Hindu Triad multiplied until there were millions of them, and the castes divided and subdivided from the original four to a very large number, so also has this extremely old religion given rise to many sects.

There are sects who worship Vishnu as the god of space and time.

There are sects who worship Shiva (or Lord Siva) as a god of song and healing.

There are sects who worship Durga, the Divine Mother (goddess of motherhood).

And there are many others. But all the various sects believe in:

Brahman, the eternal Trimutri, or Three-in-One God: *Brahma*, the Creator; *Vishnu*, the Preserver; and *Shiva*, the Destroyer;

Submission to Fate, since man is not outside, but part of Brahman;

The *Caste System*, determined by the Laws of Manu;

The *Law of Karma*, that from good must come good, and from evil must come evil;

Reincarnation, as a chain of rebirths in which each soul, through virtuous living, can rise to a higher state;

Nirvana, the final stage reached upon the emancipation of the soul from the chain of rebirths;

Yogas, the disciplines which enable the individual to control the body and the emotions; and

Dharma, the Law of Moral Order, which each individual must find and follow to reach *Nirvana*.

12. Sayings from the Bhagavad-Gita

The precepts which teach the basic beliefs of Hinduism are given throughout the voluminous literature of the *Vedas* (the sacred Books of Knowledge); the *Brahmanas,* the commentaries on the *Vedas;* the *Upanishads,* mystic speculations; the *Hitopadesa* (The Book of Good Counsel); and, particularly, the *Bhagavad-Gita,* which is part of the great epic, the *Mahabharata.*

The soul which is not moved, that takes sorrow and takes joy indifferently, lives in the life undying.

Birthless and deathless and changeless remains the spirit, dead though the house of it seems.

As one lays away a worn-out robe and takes a new one, so the spirit puts by its garment of flesh and passes to inherit a new one.

If you hear that the man newly dead is like the man newly born, will you weep? The end of birth is death; the end of death is birth: this is ordained.

Find the reward of doing right, in right.

Make your acts your piety.

Scorn those who follow virtue for her gifts.

Because they seek no gain, the right-hearted rise more certainly from the bands of body, step by step, to the highest bliss.

In sorrows not dejected, in joys not overjoyed; outside the stress of passion, fear and anger, steadfastly calm in lofty contemplation; such a one is the wise man.

He is wise who draws away his five frail senses from the world which assails them, as the tortoise draws its feet beneath the safety of its shell.

That man alone is wise who remains master of himself.

Pondering on objects of the senses gives rise to attraction; from attraction grows desire, desire flames to passion, passion breeds recklessness; and then betrayed memory lets noble purpose go, and saps the mind, till purpose, mind and man are all undone.

The mind that follows the senses sees its helm of wisdom torn away, and, like a ship in a storm, drives to wreck and death.

What seems as wakeful day to the thick night of ignorance, is known for night to the true-seeing eyes of the wise man, just as what seems midnight-gloom to unenlightened souls shines like wakeful day to his clear gaze.

He who shakes off the yoke of flesh lives as lord, not servant, of his lusts.

No man shall escape from acting by shunning action; and none shall come by mere renunciation to perfection.

Thought is act in fancy.

Do your allotted task! Work excels idleness.

Do your earthly duty free from desire, and you shall well perform your heavenly purpose.

By works alone the ancient saints reached blessedness!

It is better for one to do his own task as he may, even though he fail, than take tasks not his own, though they seem good.

To die performing duty is no ill.

The world is strong, but what discerns it stronger, and the mind strongest; and high over all the ruling soul.

To learn which work saves one must rightly meditate on these three: Doing, not doing and undoing.

He who sees how action may be rest and rest action—he is wisest among his kind; he has the truth. He does well acting or resting.

Some votaries serve the gods with flesh and altar-smoke, but others light subtler fires and make a purer rite with will of worship.

The one who makes no sacrifice, he has no part or lot even in this world.

The sacrifice which knowledge pays is better than the great gifts offered by wealth.

Knowing truth, your heart will ache no more with error.

If you were the worst of all wrong-doers, the ship of truth would bear you safe across the sea of your transgressions.

The flame of knowledge burns away the dross.

Mankind errs by folly, darkening knowledge.

The world is overcome even here by those who fix their faith on unity.

Be not overglad attaining joy, and be not oversad encountering grief.

The joys which spring from the senses breed sure grief.

As often as the wild and wavering heart breaks from control, so often recurb it and rein it back to the control of the soul.

Perfect bliss grows only in the heart made tranquil, the spirit free from passion and purged from offense.

Beyond denial man's heart is hard to restrain, and wavering; yet it grows restrained by habit, by the use of self-control.

Of many thousand mortals, one, perhaps, strives for truth.

Four sorts of mortals know Me: he who weeps, the man who yearns to know, he who toils to help and he who sits certain of Me, enlightened.

Higher, deeper, innermost, abides another life, not like the life of the senses, escaping sight, unchanging. This endures when all created things have passed away.

Whoever offers Me in faith and love a leaf, a flower, a fruit, or water poured forth, that offering made lovingly, with pious will, I accept.

Those who worship me with love, I love; they are in me, and I in them.

Be certain that none can perish, trusting Me.

You who have come into this sorrowful and fleeting world, set your faith fast on Me.

Make Me your supreme joy, and to My rest your spirits shall be guided.

Near renunciation—very near—dwells eternal peace.

He who troubles not his kind, and is not troubled by them; free of wrath, living too high for gladness, grief or fear—that man I love.

He who, fixed in faith on Me, dotes upon none, scorns none; rejoices not and grieves not, letting good or evil light when it will, and when it will, depart—that man I love.

He who, to friend and foe, keeping an equal heart, with equal mind bears shame and glory; with an equal peace takes heat and cold, pleasure and pain; abides freed of desires, hears praise or calumny in passionless restraint, unmoved by each; linked by no ties to earth, steadfast in Me—that man I love.

Know that nature and the spirit both have no beginning.

He sees indeed who sees in all alike the living, lordly soul, supreme, imperishable amid the perishing.

Ignorance, begot of darkness, blinding mortal men, binds down their souls to sloth and stupor.

Passion binds by toilsome strain; but ignorance, which shuts out the beams of wisdom, binds the soul to sloth.

The fruit of lust is pain and toil.

The fruit of ignorance is deeper darkness.

Those of little wit, dark-minded, give themselves to evil deeds.

Ensnared in nooses of a hundred idle hopes, slaves of passion and anger buy wealth with their base deeds to glut hot appetites.

The doors of hell are threefold, through which men to ruin pass—the door of lust, the door of wrath, the door of avarice.

The faith of each believer conforms itself to what he truly is.

Purity, rectitude and no injury to any helpless thing—these mark the true religious act.

Religion shown in act of proud display is rash and vain.

Being in the body, none may stand wholly aloof from acts; yet, he who abstains from profit of his acts is abstinent.

True knowledge is to see one changeless life in all the lives, and in the Separate, One Inseparable.

Right action is wrought without attachment, passionlessly, for duty, not for love, nor hate, nor gain.

Good is the intellect which comprehends what must be done, and what must not be done, what should be feared, and what should not be feared, what binds and what emancipates the soul.

Good is the steadfastness by which a man masters his heartbeats, his very breath of life, the action of his senses; fixed in never-shaken faith.

Painful pleasure springs from the bond between the senses and the sense-world. Sweet as ambrosia is its first taste, but its last is bitter as poison.

A Brahmin's virtues, born of his nature, are serenity, self-mastery, religion, purity, patience, uprightness, learning, and to know the truth of things which be.

A Kshatriya's pride, born of his nature, lives in valor, fire, constancy, skillfulness, spirit in fight, and openhandedness and noble mien, as of a lord of men.

A Vaisya's task, born with his nature, is to till the ground, tend cattle, venture trade.

A Sudra's state, suiting his nature, is to minister.

3 BUDDHISM

The Awakened

1. Prince of Lummini

Buddhism, in its purest form, is less a religion and more a philosophy of life and a system of ethics.

It arose about 2500 years ago in India at a time when the people had become deeply disillusioned with Hinduism, its multiplication of castes, and growing number of outcastes. Instead of finding solace in the accepted belief of reincarnation, they began to consider with dread the prospect of going through thousands upon thousands of lives—births and deaths and rebirths—in an almost endless cycle, before they could hope to better their lot. They saw their fate as a dark doom rather than a bright promise. And many began to seek release from the wheel of reincarnation in self-torture and self-immolation. Some turned to the worship of animals, particularly monkeys, elephants, and cows, which harked back to a much earlier phase of Animism. And a great number of sects arose.

As the vast majority of the people were illiterate and indescribably poor, the gap widened between the few literates and the host of illiterates, between the few princes and rulers and their millions of subjects, between the few privileged of high caste and the great underprivileged population that belonged to the lower castes and outcastes. This gap grew wider and wider. And from the hopelessness among the many arose despair.

In this time of growing despair the Buddha was born.

As in the case of nearly every great religious leader the story of Buddha's life was recorded after his greatness became manifest. And by then the facts of his life had already become encrusted by chroniclers and admirers with colorful legends and miraculous events. The greater the man, the more the probable and improbable legends that grow up about him. And about the Buddha the pile of recorded legends grew as if they might rival the Himalayas, in whose shadow he was born.

For a long time certain scholars even doubted whether there had ever existed an historical character behind the legends of the Buddha, just as certain scholars have doubted the historical existence of Moses, Zoroaster, and others like them. But as late as the end of the nineteenth century archaeologists discovered a pillar, erected in 250 B.C., bearing an inscription which gave proof of Buddha's existence. Other discoveries made since that time have added more proofs that Buddha did exist and made it possible to give fixed dates and the names of his parents and the places where he had lived.

In the year 563 B.C. a child was born to King Suddhodhana and Queen Maya who ruled over the Sakyas, a tribe of the Gautamas in northern India, at the foot of the Himalayas. The infant was born in the royal palace in Lummini, according to the tablet found by the archaeologists in 1896; and there he was named Siddhartha Gautama. Among the legends which have sprouted and flourished there are many

about Prince Siddhartha's parents; about his five hundred and
fifty previous incarnations; about his youthful exploits and
skills; and about his great love and compassion for all
living things.

Some of these legends were later gathered into books
which became part of the Sacred Books of Buddhism. The
Birth-Stories, known as *Jatakas,* were gathered into such a
book, since they related events in the former incarnations
of the Buddha, when he was the Bodisat: the Buddha-to-be.

Upon his twelfth birthday Prince Siddhartha put on the
Sacred Thread, which was the custom followed by Hindu
boys of his age and his caste, and he took the Vow of
Allegiance to the religion of his fathers. Then he was sent
away to the learned priests who were to teach him the
Vedas, its voluminous commentaries, and the (orally transmitted) great religious epics. At the end of four years he
returned home as versed in the Hindu sacred scriptures as
anyone in his father's kingdom.

Upon his return the young prince married the beautiful
Princess Yosodhara, and for ten years they lived surrounded
by beauty and luxury and carefully shielded from anything painful or unpleasant in the world around them.

One day, shortly after a son was born to him, the Prince
was confronted by four sights that caused a complete change
in his life.

2. The Four Sights

This, we are told, is what happened on that fateful day:

The Prince had been out hunting, carefree and happy,
and was returning with his companion to the palace when
they came upon a man lying upon the ground, writhing in
pain. The Prince asked his companion what was wrong
with the man, And he was told:

"That is the way of life. All people are liable to become
ill and suffer pain."

Farther on their way they met an old man, with back
curved, hands trembling, and head nodding. He shuffled
along using two canes to aid his unsteady steps. And when
the Prince asked what was wrong with the man, his companion explained:

"All people grow old, and that is the way of old age."

As they continued along their path, the Prince lost in
thought about the sick man and the trembling old man,
a funeral procession came toward them. Behind the man
being carried to his cremation the widow and children

followed, weeping bitterly. The Prince asked what this sorrowful procession could mean. And he was told:

"That is the way of life. Whether one is a king or a pauper, sooner to some and later to others, death comes to all alike."

The three sights shook the young Prince. Until this day he had been carefully spared the sight of illness, old age and death. He was moved by man's lot, and the impermanence of life which, for many, must be full of pain and sorrow.

As they neared the palace, a monk appeared before them with a bowl in his hand, silently begging for his food, his face calm and his manner serene.

The prince gazed thoughtfully upon the tranquil face of the monk. Then and there he made his great decision. He determined to leave his palace, his wife and newly born son, and live as a beggar-monk, so that he could meditate without distraction upon the human condition, upon pain and old age and death.

Without hesitation or delay, the Prince shaved his head, put on the rough garment of a monk, and left the palace in search of enlightenment.

The night he left his home is known in Buddhism as the Night of the Great Renunciation.

3. Under the Bo Tree

The Prince-turned-beggar wandered about from place to place for seven years in search of wisdom. He visited monasteries and discussed with other monks the truth as revealed in the *Vedas*. But he could find no answers to the questions he put during this quest for enlightenment. At times he became discouraged. But he continued. He practiced asceticism, often fasting until he fainted. He grew weaker and weaker, but no wiser. Finally he decided that self-immolation does not lead to wisdom. He began to eat and regained his strength. His mind became clearer, and he continued his search.

One day he sat down under a wild fig-tree to meditate, and he vowed not to move from that spot until he found the wisdom he was seeking. Under the tree he remained hour after hour concentrating on all he had learned in the *Vedas;* on what he accepted and what he rejected. Suddenly his face lit up with joy and he exclaimed:

"The First Law of Life is: From good must come good, and from evil must come evil. This is the Key to Wisdom."

He knew this idea was nothing new, for it was the law of Karma, taught by Hinduism. But from it he drew new conclusions. For seven days he remained under the fig-tree (now called the Bo Tree: the Tree of Wisdom) preparing to answer any questions he might be asked upon the conclusions he had reached. Then he went to the City of Benares, gathered around him a number of monks and preached to them his first sermon—forever remembered as *The Sermon at Benares.*

When he finished, according to legend, one monk asked him:

"Are you a god?"

"No," answered Gautama.

"Then, are you a saint?"

"No," came the prompt reply.

"If you are not a god and not a saint, then what are you?"

"I am awake," answered Gautama the Prince.

From that day on his disciples and followers called him: *Buddha,* which means The Awakened or The Enlightened.

The Buddha was about thirty-five years old when he became known as *The Awakened;* and his teachings, which began with *The Sermon at Benares,* started what was to become a great religion, which would find millions of followers even outside India.

The Buddha organized his missionary teachings into discourses and went out to preach them to whosoever would listen. Among the people of India, disillusioned with the traditional religious teachings, many listened eagerly to his discourses and become his followers.

4. The Spread of Buddhism

By the time the Buddha died, at the age of eighty, Buddhism had taken root and had become an effective moral force in India. And this force lasted for a thousand years. When Hinduism itself finally instituted reforms, it regained its earlier hold over the people, and the influence of Buddhism in India began to diminish. But by that time its followers had carried the message of Buddhism to Ceylon and Burma, Thailand and China, Korea and Tibet and Japan.

Each country into which Buddhism entered felt the impact of the moral force of this religion. And Buddhism, in turn, was influenced by the local conditions it encountered, changing in ritual, in the orders of the monks and nuns and in their religious ceremonies. In time many sects arose which differed in ritual and in the interpretation of the teachings of the Buddha. The basic tenets of his beliefs, however, remained unchanged and were accepted by all.

Buddhism had the virtue not only of being adaptable to the different environments into which it entered, but it also was capable of adjusting to new times and new conditions.

Today, although the sects and branches of Buddhism are many, they can be divided into two major divisions: Followers of the Greater Vehicle of Salvation *(Mahayana);* and Followers of the Lesser Vehicle of Salvation *(Hinanyana).* These divisions arose out of their differing interpretations of the Sacred Books gathered around the Buddha's teachings, to which they, themselves, liberally contributed.

Mahayana (the Greater Vehicle of Salvation) started out with an interpretation of the Buddha's teachings that was very close to that of *Hinanyana* (also called *Theravada*). But as time went on, the division between them became great, almost as great as the division today between Catholics and Unitarians or Universalists.

Followers of the Greater Vehicle believe that no man lives alone and therefore his salvation must be involved with the salvation of others. In the Lesser Vehicle, adherents believe that each individual must seek and find his own salvation.

The Greater Vehicle teaches that the principal guide of man is the heart, and "the way" is: *Compassion.* For the followers of the Lesser Vehicle, the principal guide of man is the head, and "the way" is: *Wisdom.* From this point on, the two ways grow farther apart.

Mahayana believes:
That religion is the concern of everyone;
They recognize the Buddha as a Savior;
They have a complex ritual accompanied by personal prayers.
Hinanyana believes:
That religion is the concern of monks;
They regard the Buddha as a saint and teacher;
They avoid ritual and prayer.

Each of the two major divisions and all the various sects attempt to prove the correctness of their approach by quoting the Buddha.

Buddhism has no Bible in the Judaic, Christian or Islamic sense of the word. But there is an immense collection of Buddha's sermons and sayings, as well as teachings attributed to him, and these are known as The Three Baskets of Wisdom

(*Tripitaka*). Books enough to fill a library have since been written by his disciples as commentaries and embellishments of the Buddha's teachings.

What has kept, and still keeps, Buddhism alive in the hearts of many millions of men, are the wise observations and the ethical teachings of a compassionate prince who suddenly became aware of the sorrows of mankind, and who sought to learn the meaning of their lives and how they might find salvation from the recurring cycles of reincarnation.

A favorite story is told about a woman who came to the Buddha weeping and said:

"O Enlightened One, my only son has died. I have gone everywhere asking: Is there no way to bring my son back to me? And they answered: Go to the Enlightened One. Maybe he can help you."

The Buddha looked at her compassionately and said: "If you bring me a mustard seed from a house in which neither parent, child, relative, or servant ever died, I shall bring your son back to life again."

The woman went away in search of a mustard seed from a house such as the Buddha had described. And after many months she returned.

"My daughter, have you brought the mustard seed I asked for?"

"No, I have not," she answered. "The people tell me that the living are few, but the dead are many."

Then the Buddha explained to the weeping mother the truth about suffering.

The beliefs of Buddhism are many and the interpretations vary, depending upon the particular sect, where and when they lived or live, and whether they belonged or belong to the followers of the Greater or Lesser Vehicle of Salvation.

5. The Way of the Doctrine

Today the basic beliefs of Buddhism go back to the Wise Man of the Sakyas, and begin with his recognition of the Four Noble Truths:

The First Noble Truth is that old age is suffering; illness is suffering; death is suffering; being exposed to what one dislikes is suffering; being separated from what one likes is suffering; failure to realize one's ambitions and desires is suffering.

The Second Noble Truth is that suffering comes from

the desire for being which leads from birth to rebirth, together with lust and desire, which find gratification here and there; the desire for being, the desire for pleasure and the desire for power, these are the sources of suffering.

The Third Noble Truth is that suffering can be dissolved with the complete annihilation of desire, separating oneself from it and completely expelling it.

The Fourth Noble Truth is that the cessation of all desire can be gained by following the Eightfold Path.

The Eightfold Path

Right Belief—that Truth is the guide of man;

Right Resolve—to be calm at all times and not to harm any living creature;

Right Speech—never to lie, never to slander anyone, and never to use coarse or harsh language;

Right Behavior—never to steal, never to kill, and never to do anything one may later regret or be ashamed of;

Right Occupation—never to choose an occupation that is considered bad;

Right Effort—always to strive for that which is good and avoid that which is evil;

Right Contemplation—of the Noble Truths, in calmness and detachment;

Right Concentration—will then follow and lead to the path of perfect peace.

6. The Buddhist Ten Commandments

The infallible guides on the path of perfect peace are the Buddhist Ten Commandments and the Ten Perfections.

The Buddhist Ten Commandments

1. Do not destroy life.
2. Do not take what is not given you.
3. Do not commit adultery.
4. Tell no lies and deceive no one.
5. Do not become intoxicated.
6. Eat temperately and not at all in the afternoon.
7. Do not watch dancing, nor listen to singing or plays.
8. Wear no garlands, perfumes or any adornments.
9. Sleep not in luxurious beds.
10. Accept no gold or silver.

The Ten Perfections

The first perfection is: *Giving.* As a full jar overthrown pours out the liquid and keeps back nothing, even so shall your charity be without reserve—as a jar overturned.

The second perfection is: *Duty.* As a yak-cow, when the hairs of her tail become entangled in anything, would rather suffer death than injury to her tail, even so should you keep to your duty—as the yak to her tail.

The third perfection is: *Renunciation.* As a man in prison, suffering pain for long, knows that there is no pleasure for him but only to await release, so shall you look upon your existences on earth as prisons, and turn your face toward renunciation and await release.

The fourth perfection is: *Insight.* As the beggar-monk shuns no families from whom he begs, whether lowly or high or in between, and acquires his daily fare, so shall you at all times question the wise and gain insight.

The fifth perfection is: *Courage.* As the lion, king of beasts, whether when lying down or standing up, lacks no courage, but is ever light-hearted, so also shall you in each of your individual-existences hold fast to your courage.

The sixth perfection is: *Patience.* As the earth bears all that is cast upon it, both the pure and the impure, and feels no resentment nor rejoicing, so also shall you receive favors and rebuffs alike with indifference.

The seventh perfection is: *Truth.* As the star of healing is balanced in the heavens, and swerves not from its path in its time and its season, so also shall you remain fixed on your path of truth.

The eighth perfection is: *Resolution.* As the stone mountain, firmly based, quails not before the tempest, but abides in its place, so also shall you abide in your resolution once resolved.

The ninth perfection is: *Loving-kindness.* As water quenches the thirst of the good and the bad alike, and cleanses them of dust and impurity, so also shall you treat your friend and your foe alike with loving-kindness.

The tenth perfection is: *Serenity.* As indeed the earth looks with serenity on all the pure and impure that are cast upon it, even so shall you approach with serenity both joy and sorrow—if you are to attain wisdom.

Thus many are the things which in this world make wisdom perfect; beyond these there are no others.

When he gains perfect wisdom and becomes master of himself, it is the belief of the Buddhist that he has gained salvation and is ready to enter *Nirvana.*

Nirvana is probably one of the most difficult concepts to define in a way comprehensible to the Western mind. Some have defined *Nirvana* as the state of Not-Being. This is both correct and incorrect. For *Nirvana* is a release from the cycle of reincarnation and the end of individual existence. *Nirvana* is also the blissful state in which all suffering ceases and the individual soul is joined with the World-Soul.

When one of Buddha's disciples was asked to define *Nirvana,* he thought for a while, then asked:

"Is there such a thing as wind?"

"Of course there is," came the reply.

"What is its color, its shape, its thickness?"

"It has no color or shape or thickness."

"Can one touch it and can it be shown?"

"No, it cannot be touched and it cannot be shown."

"If it cannot be shown, how do you know it exists?"

"I am positive it exists, even if it cannot be seen."

"*Nirvana* is like that," the disciple replied. "It cannot be touched, or seen. But we are positive it exists."

7. What Buddhism Believes

1. From good must come good, and from evil must come evil. This is the First Law of Life.

2. Prayers and sacrifices to the gods are useless; only understanding the Eightfold Path, and practicing the Buddhist Ten Commandments and Ten Perfections lead to perfect wisdom.

3. The *Vedas* are not sacred books since they teach that people should pray and offer sacrifices.

4. The world always was and always will be.

5. Brahma did not create people into castes out of Manu. There are, and there always were, only two kinds of people: those who are good and those who are evil.

6. The aim of life is not pleasure or happiness but the end of individual existence through the practice of the Ten Perfections.

7. He who attains perfect wisdom enters *Nirvana,* and for him the chain of reincarnation is broken.

Buddhism found many followers in many lands, particularly where the people were poor, ignorant, and hopeless. The peace and serenity offered by Buddhism and the prospect of release from pain and suffering were welcomed as a boon. And the teachings of the compassionate Buddha were embraced.

Not all the teachings as given in the Sacred Books of Buddhism were comprehensible to the majority of its followers. But all easily understood the lessons taught by the Five-Hundred-and-Fifty Birth-Stories of the Buddha * (the *Jatakas*) as found in The Three Baskets of Wisdom (the *Tripitaka*). These stories, which entertained as well as taught, concerned the Bodisat (in the reincarnations before he became the Buddha) and in which he appears many times as a king, as a teacher, as a lion, as a monkey, as a rooster, and so on.

Here is one of them:

8. The Flight of the Animals

Not far from the Bay of Bengal, in a grove of coconut palms and carob trees, lived a short-eared rabbit so timorous that he searched for food at night and rarely left his burrow in the daytime.

One day the rabbit came hesitantly out of his dwelling, looking quickly to the right and to the left of him for any sight or sign of an enemy. Reassured that there was nothing dangerous in the neighborhood, he stretched out to bask in the sun near a tall carob tree.

He lay there contentedly looking up at the oval leaves so densely interwoven that not even a pinpoint of sky could be seen through them. Here and there upon the branches hung the ripening dark-brown, sickle-shaped seed pods, swaying in the breeze. They were a pleasant sight to the rabbit, for he well knew how honey-sweet their pulp was when they began to fall to the ground.

Suddenly, as he lay there, an alarming thought struck the faint-hearted rabbit: What would happen to him if the earth began to cave in? Where would he go for safety? The more he thought of it, the more alarmed he became, until his heart nearly burst with terror.

Just then, behind his head a ripe coconut fell upon a dry palm leaf with a thundering crash. The rabbit jumped up in panic without a single look behind and scampered off as fast as his legs could carry him.

As he ran he passed a long-eared hare.

"Where are you running so fast?" called out the hare.

* Why the title of this collection of stories is given as Five-Hundred-and-Fifty is not clear, for as they now appear the number reaches well over two thousand.

But the rabbit dared not pause to answer. The hare caught up with him and ran alongside, repeating his question.

The fleeing rabbit panted: "The earth is caving in behind us!"

The hare, just as frightened, followed the short-eared rabbit, and soon they were joined by hundreds and thousands of other hares and rabbits, all trying to flee from the place where the earth was caving in.

A doe and deer in a clearing were startled by the sight of so many hares and rabbits in flight and asked the cause of their alarm. And when they were told that the earth was caving in, they too joined the stampede.

As they fled on their way, they encountered a rhinoceros, who asked the same question and received the same answer. And he, too, joined them.

Before long the stampede included bears and elks, wild oxen and gnus, jackals and monkeys, tapirs and camels, tigers, and even elephants.

A young lion at the foot of a mountain saw the animals in flight. He climbed to the top of a high rock and roared three times, his voice reverberating through the valley like a clap of thunder. All the animals stopped in their tracks. They were more frightened by the roar of their king than by the fear of the earth breaking up behind them.

"Why are you all running away?" asked the king of the beasts (who was really the Bodisat in the form of a young lion).

"The earth is caving in behind us," they all replied together.

"Who saw it caving in?" asked the lion.

"Ask the tigers, they know," replied the elephants.

But the tigers said: "We didn't see it, but the wild boars told us so."

And the wild boars said: "We didn't see it, but the camels know all about it."

And the camels pointed to the tapirs, who pointed to the deer, who pointed to the hares, who pointed to the rabbits.

When the lion questioned the rabbits one by one, he finally came to the short-eared rabbit who had started the flight of the animals.

"Are you the one who saw the earth cave in?" asked the lion, fixing his fierce eyes upon the little rabbit, who was now more terrified than ever.

"Y-y-yes, Your Majesty," stuttered the rabbit.

"Where did you see this?" asked the lion.

"Near my home, in a grove of coconut palms and carob trees. I was lying there in the sun, thinking of what would happen to me if the earth suddenly began to cave in, and just then I heard the crash of the earth breaking up right behind me. And I fled."

"Come, show me the spot where you heard the earth breaking up," said the lion.

"Your Majesty, I am afraid to go near it," said the rabbit.

"Do not fear anything when you are with me," said the lion. "Jump upon my back and I will carry you there."

Together they returned to the spot where the rabbit had basked in the sun. And there upon the palm frond the lion saw the coconut that had fallen and frightened the rabbit.

The lion returned to the other animals to tell them what he had discovered. Then each returned peacefully to his home.

But had it not been for the young lion, the Bodisat, the stampeding animals would surely have rushed into the ocean, and all would have perished.

9. Sayings from the Dhamapada

In the same *Tripitaka* there is a collection of proverbs, called The Way of the Doctrine (the *Dhamapada*), which cover the basic beliefs of Buddhism presented in a way that makes them easy to understand and easy to remember:

All that we are is the result of what we have thought: it is founded on our thoughts and is made up of our thoughts.

If a man speaks or acts with an evil thought, pain follows him, as the wheel follows the foot of the ox that draws the cart; if a man speaks or acts with a pure thought, happiness follows him, as the shadow that never leaves him.

Hatred is not diminished by hatred at any time. Hatred is diminished by love—this is the eternal law.

As rain breaks through an ill-thatched roof, so lust breaks through an ill-trained mind.

The evildoer mourns in this world, and he mourns in the next—he mourns in both. He mourns and suffers when he sees the evil results of his own deeds.

Thoughtfulness is the road to immortality (*Nirvana*); thoughtlessness, the road to death.

The thoughtful do not die; the thoughtless are as if dead already.

By thoughtfulness, by restraint and self-control, the wise man may make for himself an island which no flood can overwhelm.

Fools follow vanity; but the wise man prizes his thoughtfulness as a treasure.

If a man's faith is unstable and his peace of mind troubled, his knowledge will not be perfect.

Man, whose body is as fragile as a jar, should make his thoughts firm as a fortress.

He who knows that his body is like froth and as unsubstantial as a mirage, will break the flower-tipped arrow of the Great Tempter and never see the King of Death.

Like a beautiful flower full of color but without scent are the fair words of him who himself does not act accordingly.

The scent of flowers does not travel against the wind; but the fragrance of good people travels even against the wind.

Even upon a heap of rubbish the lotus will grow full of sweet perfume and delight; even so the true disciple of the enlightened Buddha will shine forth among the people who walk in darkness.

Long is the night to him who is wakeful; long is the mile to him who is tired; long is life to the foolish who do not know the true law.

"These sons belong to me and this wealth belongs to me"— with such thoughts the fool tries to console himself. He himself does not belong to himself, how much less his sons and wealth!

The deed of which a man must repent, and the results of which he receives with tears, is not well done; the deed which a man does not repent, and the results of which he receives with joy, is well done.

An evil deed, like freshly drawn milk, does not turn sour at once.

As long as the evil deed done does not bear fruit, the fool thinks it is like honey; but when it ripens, then he suffers.

The fool wishes for precedence among the monks, for lordship in the monasteries, for honor among other people.

If you meet a man who can show you what is to be avoided and knows how to administer reproof, follow him as you would follow a man who can reveal hidden treasures.

As a solid rock is not shaken by the wind, so the wise man does not waver before blame or praise.

If, whether for his own sake or for the sake of others, a man neither wishes for a son, nor wealth, nor leadership, and if he does not wish for any success by unfair means, he is a good and wise man.

Few there are among men who arrive at the other shore; most of them run up and down this shore.

Those whose minds are well-grounded in the seven elements of knowledge, who cling to nothing with rejoicing, who curb their appetites and are full of light, they gain *Nirvana* even in this world.

Though a man go out to battle a thousand times against a thousand men, if he conquers himself he is the greater conqueror.

Not even a god can change into defeat the victory of a man who has vanquished himself.

If a man commits a sin, let him not do it again; let him not delight in it, for the accumulation of evil is painful.

Even if the water falls drop by drop, it will fill the pot; and the fool will become full of evil, even though he gathers it little by little.

Not in the sky, not in the midst of the sea, not even in the clefts of the mountains is there a spot in the whole world where, if a man abide there, death could not overtake him.

All men tremble at punishment and all men fear death; remember that you are like them and do not kill nor cause slaughter.

Not nakedness, not matted locks, not dirt or fasting or sleeping on the bare earth, or sitting motionless can purify a man who has not overcome his doubts.

One's own self is the most difficult to subdue.

Self is the lord of self.

The pure and impure stand and fall by their own deeds; no one can purify another.

He whose evil deeds are covered by good deeds brightens up the world, like the moon when freed from clouds.

Not to blame, not to strike, to be moderate in eating, to sleep and sit alone, and to dwell on the highest thoughts—this is the teaching of the Awakened.

Men, driven by fear, go to many refuges—to the mountains, to the forests, to groves of sacred trees—but none delivers him from his pains. But he who takes refuge with Buddha who sees the Four Holy Truths and follows the Eightfold Holy Path—he will be delivered from pain.

We live happily, indeed, among men who hate us, free of hatred; among men who are greedy, free from greed. Though we call nothing our own, we shall be like the bright gods, feeding on happiness.

Victory breeds hatred. He who has given up both victory and defeat, he is contented and happy.

There is no fire like passion; there is no evil like hatred; there is no pain like this body; there is no happiness greater than peace.

He who has tasted the sweetness of solitude and tranquillity becomes free from fear and free from sin.

From pleasure come grief and fear; he who is free from pleasure knows neither grief nor fear.

Kinsmen, friends and lovers (well-wishers) salute a man

who has been away for a long time and returns safe from afar; likewise his good works receive a man when he comes from this world to the other.

No suffering befalls the man who calls nothing his own.

He who holds back rising anger like a rolling chariot is a real driver; others are but holding the reins.

Let a man overcome anger by love, let him overcome evil by good, let him overcome greed with liberality and lies with truth.

By these three steps you will come near to the gods: speak the truth; do not yield to anger; give even though you have but a little to give.

There is an old saying: they blame him who sits silent; they blame him who speaks much; they blame him who says little. There is no one in the world who does not get blamed.

Life is easy to live for a man who is without shame, bold as a crow, a mischief-maker, insulting, arrogant and dissolute. But life is hard to live for a man who is modest, always looks for what is pure, free from attachment, unassuming, and clear of vision.

You yourself must make the effort. The Buddhas are only teachers.

All created things perish; he who knows and sees this is at peace in a world of pain. All existing things in this world are unreal; he who knows and sees this is beyond the thrall of grief.

Cut down the whole forest of desire, not just one tree only.

"Here I shall dwell in the winter and summer, here I shall dwell in the rain"—so the fool thinks, but does not think of death.

If by leaving a small pleasure one sees a great pleasure, the wise man will leave the small pleasure to look at the great.

Good people shine from afar, like the peaks of the Himalayas.

The passion of a heedless man grows like a creeper, and he runs from life to life, like a monkey seeking fruit in the forest.

The gift of the Law exceeds all gifts; the sweetness of the Law exceeds all sweetness; the delight in the Law exceeds all delight; the extinction of all desire overcomes all suffering.

Without knowledge there is no meditation, without meditation there is no knowledge. He who has knowledge and meditation is near to *Nirvana*.

Long after the days of Buddha, and far away from his birthplace arose a sect of Buddhism known as Zen, which has intrigued mystics for a millennium and has now aroused enormous interest in the Western world. Zen is described in Chapter 12.

4 JAINISM

The Sky-Clad and the Blue-Clad

1. Similar but Very Different

About the time that Gautama the Buddha lived and established a new religion in India, another teacher arose who also opposed the caste system and wished to reform Hinduism. He was Prince Vardhamana, son of King Sreyama and Queen Trisala of the Kingdom of Magadah, in the north of India. He became known as *Mahavira*, which means the Great Hero.

So similar seemed the life histories and some of the teachings of these two religious reformers, that for centuries students of Indian religions thought they were one and the same person, presented under two different names; and that two different versions had been told and recorded in different localities. When later scholars scrutinized the records, they found that though the teachings of the Buddha and Mahavira began with similarities, they ended with irreconcilable differences.

And this is what they found:

About a decade or two before the birth of the Buddha, a son was born to the King and Queen of Magadah, a neighboring kingdom of the Sakyas, and he was named Vardhamana.

The young prince was brought up in the luxury of the royal palace. At an early age he was taught the use of the bow and arrow, how to manage wild horses, how to control elephants, and the other skills expected of princes at that time in India. In all of these he excelled and exhibited such unusual courage that he was given the name of *Mahavira*, the Great Hero. According to custom, at the age of twelve, Mahavira put on the Sacred Thread, which was the tradition in Hinduism for members of his caste; and he took the Vow of Allegiance to his religion. Then he was sent to study the *Vedas* and other sacred books with the priests, into whose hands his education was entrusted.

Upon returning from his studies at the age of nineteen,

he married the beautiful Princess Yosadha, and they lived happily in his father's palace for nearly ten years.

So far, except for the difference in names of people and places, the stories of Prince Gautama and Prince Vardhamana seem to be the same.

When Mahavira was twenty-nine years old, both his father and mother died. They were not assassinated. They did not meet with an accident. They did not die of a fatal disease. The King and Queen died of slow starvation. For they were very religious people, who had starved themselves so that they would die what was then considered a holy death.

Their death was such a great loss to Mahavira that he took the Vow of Silence for twelve years, and became a beggar-monk. He wandered throughout the land, meditating on the source of human suffering and the way to find salvation.

And when his Vow of Silence was fulfilled, Mahavira thought he had found the answer to life's problems. He went out to preach to the people, and those who came to hear him later said: "He was a great speaker. He spoke the truth." Before long many became his disciples.

Mahavira established a new religion, called *Jainism:* the Religion of the Conquerors. This was a new variety of "conquerors." For the *Jains,* as the followers of this religion called themselves, did not want to go out and conquer others. They only wanted to conquer themselves. Their teacher taught them: *Within yourself lies salvation.*

Like the Buddha, Mahavira began with accepting Hinduism's Law of Karma: From good must come good, and from evil, evil.

Like the Buddha, he accepted the belief in Reincarnation and the ultimate release in *Nirvana.*

But here both the Buddha and Mahavira parted company with Hinduism. Both rejected the belief in the sacredness of the caste system; salvation by prayer; and the absolute truth of the *Vedas.*

At this point the two reformers parted: The Buddha followed the Middle Path of Moderation; Mahavira turned sharply away to Asceticism.

2. The Sacredness of Life

Mahavira believed that the good life can be lived only in self-denial, because desire is the cause of all suffering.

He believed, and his followers believe, that the soul of man is eternal; that it has always existed and will always continue to exist. But he did not share the Buddha's belief that man's soul is part of the World-Soul. Mahavira preached that each man's soul is individual. He who conquers himself, conquers all that is worth conquering. And the conquest of oneself can be accomplished through self-denial, through asceticism, through austere renunciation of all desire, of all worldly ambitions, which are only mirages that deceive.

"It is difficult to conquer oneself," said Mahavira, "but when that is conquered, everything is conquered."

The conquest of oneself begins with the strict and difficult discipline of one's desires—it begins with stringent self-denial. Yet self-denial is only the negative side, the "thou shalt not" side, of self-conquest. If this alone is followed, it leads to frustration. The positive side to this conquest is the right conduct toward, and consideration of, others. And by others Mahavira meant, not only human beings, but *all things that live*.

This concept of consideration toward all things that live became the core and center of Mahavira's belief and teachings. He called it *Ahimsa*, which means "non-injury" but implies a reverence for life and the living. All his teachings have been identified and summed up with this one word: *Ahimsa*. All the rest were elaborations.

Mahavira classified the consequences of *Ahimsa* and arranged them into orderly doctrines. He taught that a man's soul is purified and grows lighter when obeying the Divine Law of Life. And when it is burdened with sin, it becomes heavy. The saintlier a soul, the higher it rises. And if a soul becomes so light that it ascends above the twenty-six heavens, which rise one above the other, then it reaches *Nirvana*. But the sin-burdened soul will sink down into hell. And if the sins are many, the soul will sink to the lowest of the seven hells that lie below each other.

Mahavira taught his doctrines to the people for thirty years, and instructed them how they might achieve the goodness of heart that would bring them above the uppermost heaven to their goal of *Nirvana*.

3. The Precepts of Jainism

After the death of Mahavira, his disciples gathered his sermons into forty-six books, called *Agamas*, meaning Precepts. And the *Agamas* became the sacred scriptures of Jainism.

Foremost among the Jainist sacred books are the Twelve *Angas*. The second *Anga*, called *Sutra-Krit-Anga*, contains a number of sayings or proverbs which underscore the Jainist beliefs. The following precepts are based on the Hermann Jacobi translations from the Pakrit:

Know what causes the bondage of the soul; and knowing, try to remove it.

All things are eternal by their very nature.

As imprisoned birds do not get out of their cage, so those ignorant of right or wrong do not get out of their misery.

There are three ways of committing sins: by our actions; by authorizing others, and by approval.

A sage leads a life as far removed from love as from hate.

All living beings hate pain: therefore do not injure them or kill them. This is the essence of wisdom: not to kill anything.

Leave off pride, anger, deceit and greed.

Men suffer individually for the deeds they themselves have done.

The wise man should consider that not he alone suffers; all creatures in the world suffer.

Conceit is a very thin thorn; it is difficult to pull out.

No man should seek fame and respect by his austerities.

A man should treat all creatures in the world as he himself would like to be treated.

He who is purified by meditation is like a ship in the water that avoids all dangers until it reaches the shore.

Do not maintain that there is no such thing as good or evil, but that there is good and evil.

4. The Swatambara and the Digambara

As time went on, and the followers of Jainism increased, they became divided into two sects: The *Swatambara,* whose priests are clad in white; and the *Digambara,* whose priests are "sky-clad"—wearing only loincloths.

Their differences are mainly doctrinal. But both sects adhere to the Five Commandments of the Soul, given to them by Mahavira. They are:

1. Do not kill any living thing; do not hurt any living thing by word, thought or deed—even in self-defense.
2. Do not steal.
3. Do not lie.
4. Do not live an unchaste life. Do not become intoxicated.
5. Do not covet or desire anything.

The most important of these is the First Commandment, which became the cornerstone of Jainism. The other four commandments Jains share with other religions and with other ethical codes. The first commandment has become the differentiation and crown of Jainism.

To observe the first commandment in the spirit in which it was given to them, Jains became vegetarians. They never eat meat, even when it is a question of health or survival.

In time of war, Jains are noncombatants. Through the centuries they have been opposed to war. And when a war comes, though they will go in as medical workers, stretcher-bearers, or on any mercy missions however dangerous, they will not bear arms.

Jains obviously cannot become butchers. Neither can they become farmers, for in plowing the soil they might kill worms, and worms are a form of life—and all forms of life must be held sacred. By the same token they cannot engage in fishing, or in any other occupation in which life in any form is endangered.

As a result of the belief in *Ahimsa,* Jains become monks or teachers, artists or traders, businessmen or bankers. As a rule they are more educated than their neighbors in India, more prosperous, and more influential. Yet it is against their religion for them to exploit their advantages for themselves.

Next in importance to *Ahimsa* is the Jainist belief in self-denial. The Jains are ascetics. No matter how rich a man may be, he must not indulge his desires, as a matter of self-discipline. "Virtuous men regard pleasures as equal to diseases," states their *Sutra-Krit-Anga.* "A pious man eats little, drinks little, sleeps little." These are disciplines of self-denial.

The third basic belief of Jainism is charity, though the Jains do not call it "charity." They consider it their duty to share with others and to take care of others.

They maintain hospitals; care for the sick; give aid to the orphaned, the widowed, the injured. They also have hospitals for sick animals, particularly cows. Their religion demands many things of them which they must perform daily. First of these is the carrying out of at least one act of charity each day.

Yet the Jains, who are so considerate of anything and everything that is alive, tolerate suicide in old age. For they believe that death by starvation is a holy death.

The Jains, and particularly those who belong to the Orthodoxy, the *Digambara,* believe that women cannot enter *Nirvana.* However, if women lead chaste and good lives, practice charity and learn to conquer themselves, after several incarnations they may be reincarnated as men. Then, along with men, they can find the way to *Nirvana* through the Three Jewels of the Soul:

Right Conviction,

Right Knowledge, and

Right Conduct.

In the sacred books of the Jains it is written that this religion is meant for all mankind, that it is a universal religion. But Mahavira's teachings never took root outside of India, never found a following outside of its birthplace. Even there its following has never been great and is now dwindling. In India today there are only about one and a half million Jains. Yet the Jainist beliefs in generosity, humility, personal responsibility for all in need, and dedication to peace can certainly inspire the ethical aspirant in any society.

Though Jainists believe that *Nirvana* is not reached through prayers but through good deeds and the right conduct, they do have many temples, and they pray to the twenty-four Jinas, of which Mahavira was the twenty-fourth and last. They do not pray for health or wealth, they do not pray for honor in the eyes of men or for success in their professions. They only pray for the gift of *Nirvana:*

> To the Lord Jinandra, Shri Shanti,
> The worshiped of all the world,
> The Giver of Peace and Joy,
> I bow down my humble head.
> Peace eternal may he award
> To all the beings on earth.
> May I obtain by his favor
> The Highest gift of *Nirvana.*

5. The Sayings of Jainism

All things are eternal by their very nature.

As imprisoned birds do not get out of their cage, so those ignorant of right or wrong do not get out of their misery.

Misery arises from wicked deeds.

The world is boundless and eternal; it exists for eternity and shall not perish.

Men suffer individually for the deeds they themselves have done.

The wise man should consider that not he alone suffers; all creatures in the world suffer.

The wise man who can see far into the past and the future will practice indifference.

Knowing the truth, one should live up to it.

The fool thinks that his wealth, cattle and kin will save him; they him, or he them.

If you are intent on your spiritual welfare, do not kill

any living beings by your acts, by your orders, or by your consent.

A man considers himself a hero as long as he does not behold the foe.

If you hold fast to what is wrong, you will regret it, like the man who carried iron a long way believing it was silver.

They who spend much time with women cease to practice meditation.

As thunder is the loudest of sounds, as the moon is the most glorious of heavenly bodies, and as sandalwood is the best of perfumes, so is he who has renounced all desires.

Reckless men who cut down sprouts out of regard for their own pleasure, destroy many living creatures.

No man should seek fame and respect by his austerities.

A wise man should abstain from: fame, glory, and renown; honors, respectful treatment, and all pleasures of this world.

The foolish man is full of selfishness; he toils day and night, greedy for wealth, as if he will never grow old or die.

A blind man, though he may carry a light, still does not see.

He who is carried away by passion will not get very far.

He who knows the truth is kind to his fellow creatures.

He who recognizes that he sins and does not cease from sinning is called a foolish man.

There were three hundred and sixty-three philosophical schools, and their founders differed in intellect, will, character, taste, understanding and plans; and all formed into one circle and each one stood in his place. Then a man, carrying with a pair of iron tongs a vessel full of burning coals, asked the philosophers to take the vessel from him with their bare hands for only a moment. But the philosophers held back, because they said, if they took it their hands would burn and cause them pain. Then said the man, "This is a maxim of general application, a true principle of religious reflection: all creatures are averse to pain. They who cause pain to any creature will in time-to-come suffer a variety of pains."

5 CONFUCIANISM

The Middle Path

1. Three Times Three

The great religions of the world may be divided into three groups of three:

The religions that originated in India: *Hinduism; Buddhism;* and *Jainism;*

The religions that originated in China and Japan: *Confucianism; Taoism;* and *Shinto;* and

The religions that originated in the Near East: *Judaism; Christianity;* and *Islam.*

Added to these there are other faiths, some ancient and some of recent birth, which are amalgamations of Hinduism and Islam, of Buddhism and Christianity, of Buddhism and Confucianism, and many other combinations and variations of the three principal groups. But all the beliefs are based on, or derived from, these three groups. In the last three centuries the faiths and sects tended to multiply; in our day they tend to coalesce rather than to break up into new faiths and sects.

In the religions of India the beliefs can be characterized as philosophical, introspective, exploring the nature of ultimate reality; and, to the Western mind, frustratingly pessimistic.

In the Near-Eastern religions the beliefs are basically moralistic; self-assertive; allowing for, or assuming, an intimate God-Man relationship; eschatological; redemptive; and optimistic.

In China and Japan the religious beliefs hardly fit into the Western concept of worship, or the search for an ultimate purpose, or individual salvation linked to a Divine Being. The followers of these beliefs are primarily traditionalists, accepting ancestor-worship, and seeking in the records of the past a guide for their behavior in the present. Their ideal is neither piety nor asceticism, but propriety and courage.

For thousands of years the Chinese were Nature-Worshipers. They believed that at some undefined beginning *P'an Ku,* the First Man, was created. *P'an Ku* set the Sun and the Moon and the Stars in the heavens; then he called the Unicorn, the Dragon, the Phoenix, the Tortoise, and the

White Tiger to help him rule the earth. When *P'an Ku* died, his last groan became the thunder; his last breath became the wind; the blood in his veins became the rivers; his hair became the forests; and his body became the earth. And the Chinese worshiped the spirits of thunder and wind, of rivers and forests, and all the other spirits of nature.

They also worshiped the spirits of their ancestors who dwelled on the stars. And in time a rigid and noble tradition grew up around their nature worship and ancestor worship. They built temples to nature-deities and ancestral-spirits; they defined the sacrifices that should be made to each of the gods to propitiate them; and created the songs and prayers to accompany the ritual observances.

The Chinese people, sensitive and imaginative, developed a rich culture of folk songs; rites and ceremonies; mystical triagrams and hexagrams whose original meaning has long been lost; histories of the Empire and its dynasties; classic poetry in hymns and festival songs.

The accumulated folklore, grown vast and complex, was in a chaotic state, and required definition and organization. It needed the right man or men to winnow the wheat from the chaff; to explain what was not clear and to discard what was no longer of value, bringing early Chinese culture into a comprehensible system.

And such a man arose. Though he called himself "a lover of the ancients," and an editor of the cultural inheritance they had left behind them, the people called him the First Teacher and Philosopher. By "first teacher" they did not mean first in order, but first in excellence. They not only honored him but, in time, they reverenced and deified him.

2. The Great Teacher K'ung

The same century that produced the Buddha and Mahavira in India (the sixth century B.C.) produced Ch'iu K'ung, son of Shu-liang Heih in China. He was not of princely birth or a son of the nobility. Although legend many years later claimed he was of royal descent and ascribed to his father superhuman feats of strength and courage in battle, Ch'iu K'ung himself, in recalling his childhood for his disciples, told then that when he was young he was "without rank and in humble circumstances."

Ch'iu was born in 551 B.C., in the District of Tsow in the province of Lu, the youngest of twelve children. He had, it is believed, an older brother. But about him nothing is known, for nothing about him is recorded anywhere; and the other children in the family did not really count for much in the China of nearly 2500 years ago, because they were girls.

When Ch'iu was only three years old, his father died, leaving the family destitute. The mother valiantly struggled to support herself and her large family and, as soon as Ch'iu was old enough, to give her last-born a good education. For a good education two things are required: good educators and good students. Ch'iu, to his mother's delight, proved to be an exceptional student. Not only did he absorb knowledge like a sponge; but he learned early how to turn disadvantages into advantages.

Ch'iu K'ung had two great disadvantages: the times he was born in; and the poverty he was born into. The times were evil. The feudal state of Lu was torn by successive wars between tyrannous overlords; and the poor were overwhelmed by despair and hopelessness. K'ung determined very early to devote himself to the study of how peaceful and honest government might be attained; and how the ignorant and the poor could be educated and trained in skills so that they would be able to live in honor and dignity.

Even as a child he loved all that was traditional and ancient. He listened in fascination to the stories his mother loved to tell about the Immortals. He bowed ceremoniously to those to whom honor was due, since bowing, he had been taught, was part of politeness and worship. And early in his education he began to delve into the ancient Chinese classics which taught the rites and ceremonies of the past.

He married at the age of eighteen, and his home soon became a meeting place for students and scholars attracted by K'ung's vast knowledge, his profound understanding, his brilliant interpretation of any topic he expounded, and the remarkable gift he had of summing up topics in memorable epigrams. He began to be called K'ung-fu-tse (K'ung the Philosopher), from which we get the name Confucius.

Confucius resigned from his government post in his early twenties and devoted himself to his studies, earning a living for himself and his family as a teacher. His fame as a teacher spread throughout the province of Lu. And according to legend, when he was in his thirties he had over three thousand pupils and followers, among them the sons of dukes and ministers. But he also had many students who were of humble origin and poor. "I have never refused to give instruction to anyone," he later told his disciples. If students were poor, he remembered his own early poverty and welcomed them. He taught the poor and rich, commoners and noblemen alike. But he would not tolerate stupidity, or a lack of enthusiasm for education in his students. "If a student was not eager," he later explained his educational method, "I did not begin to open up the subject for him. And if he was unable to state his own views, I did not try to help him out. When I had opened a topic to him, if he did not come back to me having himself worked out the rest, I did not trouble to see him again."

In all students who were eager to follow him, he instilled a love for poetry, a sense of courage, regard for justice, and veneration for tradition. He taught them, too, to be good listeners and observers. He often repeated: "Hear much, and reject what is doubtful; see much, and leave alone what is questionable." He stressed the need to question anything that was ambiguous, until the ambiguity had been dissolved. "Study without thought is a snare," he told them, "as thought without study is a danger."

3. The Five K'ing

While he taught, Confucius went on with his own studies, a habit he had developed from his early student days. He collected ancient manuscripts, he edited them and wrote commentaries on them, making the obscure comprehensible and deleting the incomprehensible. Then he arranged them into four books.

The first book, of the most ancient records, contained a collection of eight triagrams and sixty-four hexagrams which consisted solely of broken and unbroken lines. It was believed that these lines had great meaning, if one could discover the key to them. This book is known as The Book of Changes (or the *Yi K'ing*). "If I had fifty years to study the *Yi*," Confucius wrote, "I might come to be free from serious error."

Here is an example of one of the hexagrams, the *Li Hexagram* found in The Book of Changes:

The meaning of this hexagram, according to the theory of symbols, if put into words, would fill a small volume.

(1) The first line (by its position and because it is un-

broken) signifies that the subject is treading his accustomed path; if he should go forward, there will be no error.

(2) The second line (by its position and because it is unbroken) signifies that the subject, treading a path that is level and even, is a quiet and solitary man, who, if he remains firm and holds to propriety, will gain good fortune.

(3) The third line (from the bottom up, by its position and because it is broken) signifies a one-eyed man who thinks he can see; a lame man who thinks he can walk; one who treads on the tail of a tiger and is bitten. It indicates ill fortune.

(4) The fourth line (by its position and because it is unbroken) shows its subject treading on the tail of the tiger. Though he is full of apprehensive caution, he will come in the end to good fortune.

(5) The fifth line (by its position and because it is unbroken) signifies that its subject treads resolutely. And though he is firm and determined, there will be peril for him.

(6) And the sixth line (by its position and because it is unbroken) signifies that we must look at the entire course followed and examine the forebodings. If it is complete and without failure, it will lead to good fortune.

Innumerable claims have been made about these mystic diagrams, including the claim the Confucius invented some of them himself. They are today revered as sacred symbols.

In the second book he gathered together fragments on the history of five preceding dynasties. Since Confucius considered the knowledge and understanding of the history of the ancients a prerequisite for the superior man, he devoted himself to welding the fragments into a meaningful history of the past. This book is known as The Book of Annals (or the *Shu K'ing*).

The third book was a great collection of classic poetry. For Confucius believed that poetry ennobles a man; and that one who read poetry daily would do no wrong. He selected three hundred from several thousand ancient poems on topics that Confucius felt were "well fitted to rouse the mind, assist observation, make people sociable, arouse virtuous indignation." The manageable treasury to which these poems were reduced was called The Book of Odes (or *K'ing Shih*).

The fourth was The Book of Ceremonies (or *Li K'ing*). The right thing must be done in the right way, he taught. And the superior man ought to recognize that the right act should be carried out in the right or traditional way, and that the ritual or ceremony is not an embellishment but itself part of the act. Confucius was aware of the danger which existed in the possibility of accepting the ritual or ceremony while neglecting the essence of it. Against this he continually warned his disciples.

To these four books he added a fifth of his own, which was an attempt to bring the historic record up to his time. This book is called Autumn and Spring (or *Ch'un Ch'in*).

On these five books, known as the *Five K'ing*, Confucius worked throughout his lifetime. He was constantly revising, polishing, clarifying and changing them. And they were the core and central part of his teachings.

With the *Five K'ing* as texts, he taught his disciples:

Principles of courage and prudence;

The value of education and self-criticism;

The principles of filial duty;

The principles of selecting friends;

The principles of good human relations; and

The principles of good government.

4. The Case of the Successful Failure

The people of Chung-tu in the province of Lu came to Confucius when he was in his early fifties and asked him to become Chief Magistrate of their city. Confucius accepted, eager to prove that what he taught in theory would prove true in practice. After one year in office he introduced so many reforms that the city of Chung-tu became known throughout the province for its successful institutions and the happiness of its citizens.

This brought the Governor of Lu to Confucius to find out how so much had been accomplished in so short a time. Confucius explained that all he did was to reward the good and punish the bad; thus the good stayed good, and the bad became good. He also taught the people to be loyal to each other; and those who are loyal to each other are loyal to the government.

The Governor wanted to know how he had made the people happy. By choosing wise people as their teachers, Confucius told him. Even if the people did not always understand their teachers, they respected them and followed their advice.

"What you have done in the city of Chung-tu, can it be applied to the entire province of Lu?" asked the Governor.

"Even to the entire empire," Confucius replied.

The Governor then invited Confucius to become Minister of Justice for the province of Lu, where the prisons were full to overflowing and the officials did not know what to do.

The first thing Confucius did after he took office was to make a study of the prisons and their inmates. Then he called together the legislators and judges of Lu and presented to them the results of his inquiries. The vast majority of the prisoners, he had found, were ignorant and poor people, or the children of the ignorant and the poor. The rich usually had an education and the skills with which to earn a good livelihood; and when the rich committed a crime, they could evade the judgment against them by corrupting the judges. The task in Lu, Confucius concluded, was to banish ignorance through education. Then useful trades could be taught to the poor, and crime would diminish.

"But where should we begin?" asked the legislators and the judges.

"Begin with yourselves," said Confucius. "You are their legislators and judges. Do not pervert justice, having one judgment for the poor and another for the rich. The first rule of your conduct should be: Do not do anything to others that you would not want them to do to you if you were in their place."

Two years later the prisons of Lu were empty. The ideas of Confucius had proven just as wise in practice as they were in theory.

What had happened in Lu became known throughout the empire. The rogues and knaves, who profited from crime and corruption and the perversion of justice, convened in secret and plotted to rid themselves of Confucius. They knew they could not corrupt the Great Teacher, so they found a way to reach and corrupt the Governor of Lu. Before long the prisons of Lu were filled again, and Confucius went away broken-hearted.

For a number of years he wandered from province to province in search of a just governor who would give him the opportunity to put his theories of good government into practice. But he sought without success. Finally he returned home to devote his last years to the completion of the *Five K'ing*.

5. The First Sage of China

After the death of Confucius, at the age of seventy-two, his former students and disciples gathered together and decided to assemble all the sayings of their teacher which they could remember, as a memorial to his name and as a record of his methods of teaching; his Doctrines of the Middle-Path; and his ideas of government. They looked upon their Great Teacher as an educator and a statesman, a philosopher and a traditionalist, and as such they recorded him, to keep his memory and his ideas alive.

They did not consider him a religious leader. Not that he was irreligious. All his teachings had been directed to the disciplines and behavior of what he called "the superior man," and he told his disciples that "He who does not recognize the existence of a Divine Law cannot be a superior man." But he refused to discuss Heaven or the Life Hereafter. And when a disciple asked his advice upon how to celebrate a service to the spirits, he replied: "You have not yet learned how to serve man well, how can I teach you to serve the spirits?" And when asked about death and the Hereafter, he replied: "You do not yet know much about life, how can I teach you about death?"

In the discourses with his disciples Confucius never discussed religion. He taught them ethics, and these ethical teachings his disciples recorded as faithfully as they could. Though his disciples and their successors kept the memory of Confucius alive among themselves, his fame slowly began to wane among the people generally.

Then, a century after the Great Teacher died, a child was born in the same province that had been the birthplace of Confucius, and he was named Mang. At an early age Mang showed an aptitude for mimicry.

According to legend, one day his widowed mother, who lived near a cemetery, found her young son mingling with the mourners and imitating the scenes he witnessed. "This is no place for my son," said his mother. And she moved to a house near a market place. But soon she found little Mang running among the market stalls and mimicking the hawkers and their customers. "This is no place for my son," said his mother. And she moved near a school. Before long little Mang was imitating the scholars and practicing politeness. And there the mother decided to remain.

Very early in his life Mang became interested in the teachings of Confucius. He set himself the task of reviving an interest in them, and gathered about him many students to whom he taught the wisdom of the Great Teacher. The students began to call Mang, Mang the Philosopher (Mang-tze), from which we get the name Mencius.

Mencius was a good organizer and proselytizer. Wherever he went he made converts. He gathered the discourses and sayings of Confucius as recorded by the disciples, and organized them into books, the best-known of which is The Book of Analects. He went out among the people to teach the essential goodness of man's nature, as taught by Confucius. But the teachings had already assumed a religious nature, and

Confucius began to be regarded as the Teacher of a new religion.

The people were taught six principles:

1. Human nature is good; and evil is essentially unnatural;

2. Man is free to conduct himself as he wills, and he is the master of his choice;

3. Virtue is its own reward. If one does good for a reward, or avoids evil for fear of punishment—that is not virtue.

4. The rule for individual behavior is: what you do not want others to do to you, do not do to them.

5. A man has five duties: to his ruler, to his father, to his wife (and she to him); to his elder brother; to his friend. And the most important of these is the filial duty.

6. Man should strive to become a superior man.

When the rulers of the Empire asked Mencius for the essentials of his teachings, he would reply:

"What I teach is nothing new. The Master Confucius taught it before me. A just ruler governs his people according to the Five Constant Virtues. And these are:

"1. *Benevolence*, which is always to think first of what is good for the people;

"2. *Righteousness*, which is not to do to your subjects what you would not want them to do to you if you were in their place;

"3. *Propriety*, which is always to behave with courtesy and respect toward your subjects;

"4. *Wisdom*, which is to be guided by knowledge and understanding; and

"5. *Sincerity*, which is to be sincere and truthful in all you do."

The fame of Confucius grew greater in the land than at any time when the Great Teacher had been alive. And he became widely known as the First Sage of China. Mencius is remembered as the Second Sage of China.

About a hundred and fifty years following the death of Mencius, the new Emperor of China, who was a young boy, became enraged by the teachings of Confucius as taught by his disciple Mencius. He ordered all his books burned and all the scholars who knew these books orally to be driven out of the country.

The people, however, loved the teachings of Confucius and they kept his memory alive in their hearts. As soon as the Emperor died, the eminence of the First Sage became greater than ever. Sacrifices were offered to his memory, and his works were canonized. Later he was given the rank of an earl, and still later this was raised to the rank of an emperor. The people began to venerate and worship him as a god. Temples were built where he could be worshiped. And Confucianism became a religion.

6. Sayings from the Analects

The Book of Analects (*Lun Yu*) contains the sayings of Confucius and presents his ethical principles.

Men of superior mind busy themselves first getting at the root of things; when they succeed, the right course is open to them.

One excellent way to practice the rules of propriety is to be natural.

When truth and right go hand in hand, a statement will bear repetition.

Sorrow not because men do not know you; but sorrow that you do not know men.

To govern simply by statute and to maintain order by means of penalties is to render the people evasive and devoid of a sense of shame.

If you observe what people take into their hands, observe the motives, note what gives them satisfaction; then will they be able to conceal from you what they are?

When you know a thing, maintain you know it; when you do not, acknowledge it. This is the characteristic of knowledge.

Let the leader of men promote those who have ability, and instruct those who have it not, and they will be willing to be led.

To see what is right and not to do it, that is cowardice.

The superior man is not contentious. He contends only as in competitions of archery; and when he wins he will present his cup to his competitor.

A man without charity in his heart, what has he to do with ceremonies? A man without charity in his heart, what has he to do with music?

He who has sinned against Heaven has none other to whom his prayer may be addressed.

Tell me, is there anyone who is able for one whole day to apply the energy of his mind to virtue? It may be that there are such, but I have never met with one.

If we may learn what is right in the morning, we should be content to die in the evening.

The scholar who is intent upon learning the truth, yet is ashamed of his poor clothes and food, is not worthy to be discoursed with.

The superior man thinks of his character; the inferior man thinks of his position; the former thinks of the penalties for error, and the latter, of favors.

One should not be greatly concerned at not being in office, but rather about the requirements in one's self for that office. Nor should one be greatly concerned at being unknown, but rather with being worthy to be known.

The superior man seeks what is right, the inferior one what is profitable.

The superior man is slow to promise, prompt to fulfill.

Virtue dwells not in solitude; she must have neighbors.

In my first dealings with a man, I listen to his avowals and trust his conduct; after that I listen to his avowals and watch his conduct.

These are the four essential qualities of the superior man: he is humble, he is deferential to superiors, he is generously kind, and he is always just.

Those who are willing to forget old grievances will gradually do away with resentment.

I have not yet seen the man who can see his errors so as inwardly to accuse himself.

Where plain naturalness is more in evidence than fine manners, we have the country man; where fine manners are more in evidence than plain naturalness, we have the townsman; where the two are equally blended we have the ideal man.

Better than the one who knows what is right is he who loves what is right.

To prize the effort above the prize, that is virtue.

What you find in me is a quiet brooder and memorizer, a student never satiated with learning, an unwearied monitor to others.

These things weigh heavily upon my mind: failure to improve in the virtues, failure in discussion of what is learned, inability to walk always according to the knowledge of what is right and just, inability to reform what has been amiss.

Fix your mind on truth; hold firm to virtue; rely upon loving-kindness; and find your recreation in the Arts.

With coarse food to eat, water to drink, and a bent arm for a pillow, happiness may still be found.

Let there be three men walking together, and in them I will be sure to find my instructors. For what is good in them I will follow; and what is not good I will try to modify.

Sift out the good from the many things you hear, and follow them; sift out the good from the many things you see and remember them.

Without a sense of proportion, courtesy becomes oppressive; calmness becomes bashfulness; valor becomes disorderliness; and candor becomes rudeness.

Even if a person were adorned with the gift of the Duke of Chau, if he is proud and avaricious, all his other qualities are not really worth looking at.

Learn as if you could never overtake your subject, yet as if apprehensive of losing it.

When you have erred, be not afraid to correct yourself.

It is easier to carry off the chief commander of an army than to rob one poor fellow of his will.

We know so little about life, how can we then know about death?

If a man can subdue his selfishness for one full day, everyone will call him good.

When you leave your house, go out as if to meet an important guest.

Do not set before others what you yourself do not like.

The essentials of good government are: a sufficiency of food, a sufficiency of arms, and the confidence of the people. If forced to give up one of these, give up arms; and if forced to give up two, give up food. Death has been the portion of all men from of old; but without the people's trust, nothing can endure.

A tiger's or a leopard's skin might be a dog's or a sheep's when stripped of its hair.

Hold fast to what is good and the people will be good. The virtue of the good man is as the wind; and that of the bad man, as the grass. When the wind blows, the grass must bend.

Knowledge of man, that is wisdom.

The superior man feels reserved in matters which he does not understand.

Let the leader show rectitude in his personal character, and things will go well even without directions from him.

Do not wish for speedy results nor trivial advantages; speedy results will not be far-reaching; trivial advantages will matter only in trivial affairs.

The superior man will be agreeable even when he disagrees; the inferior man will be disagreeable even when he agrees.

Confucius was asked, "Is a good man one who is liked by everybody?" He answered, "No." "Is it one who is disliked by everybody?" He answered, "No. He is liked by all the good people and disliked by the bad."

In a country of good government, the people speak out boldly and act boldly.

Good men speak good words, but not all who speak good words are good. Good men are courageous, but not all courageous men are good.

It is as hard to be poor without complaining as to be rich without becoming arrogant.

The superior men are sparing in their words and profuse in their deeds.

My great concern is not with men who do not know me, but with men who cannot understand me.

Confucius was asked, "What say you of the remark, 'Repay enmity with kindness'?" And he replied, "How then would you repay kindness? Repay kindness with kindness, and enmity with justice."

Not to teach a man who can be taught, is to waste a man; to teach a man who cannot be taught, is to waste words. The wise will lose neither men nor words.

A workman who wants to do his work well must first prepare his tools.

I have not yet met the man who loves virtue as he loves beauty.

Confucius was asked, "Is there one word that sums up the basis of all good conduct?" And he replied, "Is not 'reciprocity' that word? What you yourself do not desire do not put before others."

Not to retract after committing an error is in itself an error.

The superior man may not be conversant with petty details, yet can be entrusted with important matters; the inferior man may be conversant with petty details yet cannot be entrusted with important matters.

Three things the superior man guards against: lust of the flesh in youth, combativeness in maturity, and ambition in old age.

Only the supremely wise and the abysmally ignorant do not change.

Does Heaven ever speak? The four seasons come and go, and all creatures thrive and grow. Does Heaven ever speak!

What harm can a man do to the sun or the moon by wishing to stop either in its course? It only shows that he knows not his own limitations.

Confucius was asked, "What say you are the essentials of good government?" He answered, "The ruler should esteem the five excellences and avoid the four evils. The five excellences are: plenitude without extravagance; taxation without exciting discontent; desire without covetousness; dignity without haughtiness; majesty without fierceness. The four evils to be avoided are: without instruction in the law, to inflict punishment—that is tyranny; without proper warning to expect perfect adherence—that is oppression; late in giving orders and expecting early obedience—that is robbery; to tax and to spend in a stingy manner—that is a misuse of government function."

He who does not recognize the existence of a Divine Law cannot be a superior man.

6 TAOISM

The Way

'1. The Strange Interview

In India, during the sixth century B.C., Prince Siddhartha Gautama of the Kingdom of the Sakyas, who became known as the Buddha (the Enlightened One), and Prince Vardhamana of the neighboring Kingdom of Magadah, who became known as Mahavira (the Great Hero), were contemporaries and each became the founder of a lasting religion.

In China, during the same century, Ch'iu K'ung, who became known as K'ung-fu' tse, or K'ung the Philosopher, whom we call Confucius, and another sage, about whose origin and personal life we know practically nothing, except that he was known as Lao-tze (the Old Philosopher), were also the founders of two influential yet contradictory religions, or rather, ethical codes. But while we have no record of the Buddha having ever met Mahavira, or that they had even heard of each other, there is a record or a report of a strange, and strained, meeting between Confucius and Lao-tze.

When Confucius was still a young man, although already widely known for his knowledge and humanist teachings, he received reports that an old archivist, in the Imperial Library, known as Lao-tze, was expounding strange metaphysical doctrines. Confucius, who had always been disturbed by the unusual, the inscrutable and the enigmatic, decided to meet Lao-tze the first chance he had, and learn more about these mystical teachings. Some time later Confucius wished to examine certain ancient manuscripts in the Imperial Library, and he sent word to Lao-tze, requesting an audience with him.

Confucius put on his most formal and elaborate gown for the occasion, out of politeness to his elder, and in accord with tradition. But this elaborate gown seemed to annoy Lao-tze as soon as they met.

Their interview, according to the report Confucius later made to his disciples, was as enigmatic as the hostility shown by Lao-tze. Confucius had prepared a number of questions he wished to ask of Lao-tze concerning his doctrines. But before he could even begin on the topic, Lao-tze questioned Confucius about his interests.

Confucius replied that he was interested in the history of the Ancients, especially as recorded in The Book of Annals (*Shu K'ing*).

"The men of whom you speak are long since dead and their bones are turned to ashes in their graves," Lao-tze interrupted.

Their talk continued, with Lao-tze asking the questions and Confucius answering them deferentially and politely. It was his belief, Confucius explained, that man is by nature good, and that knowledge can keep him good.

"But why study the Ancients?" Lao-tze asked impatiently.

Confucius tried to explain his belief that new knowledge must be based upon old knowledge.

Lao-tze interrupted him, saying: "Put away your polite airs and your vain display of fine robes. The wise man does not display his treasure to those he does not know. And he cannot learn justice from the Ancients."

"Why not?" asked Confucius.

"It is not bathing that makes the pigeon white," was Lao-tze's reply. And he abruptly ended the interview.

When Confucius reported the gist of the encounter to his disciples, they pressed him for his opinion of Lao-tze.

Confucius remained thoughtful for a while. Then he replied: "I know how the birds fly, how the fish swim, and how animals run. And the runners may be snared, the fish may be hooked, and the birds may be shot down with arrows. But there is the dragon. I cannot tell how it mounts the wind and ascends above the clouds. I have seen and talked with Lao-tze, and I can only compare him with the dragon." And he would say no more.

In his Introduction to the *Tao Teh King*, James Legge, famed British translator of the monumental *Chinese Classics* as given in the *Sacred Books of the East*, states:

The two men [Confucius and Lao-tze] seem to have met more than once, and I am inclined to think that the name of Lao-tze, as the designation of the other, arose from Confucius' styling him to his disciples as "the Old Philosopher." They met as Heads of different schools or schemes of thought; but did not touch, as far as we know, on the comparative antiquity of their views.

Other sources, too, state, or imply, that there was a meeting between these philosophers, whose doctrines were so different.

2. Who Was the Old Philosopher?

Nothing is known about Lao-tze's parents, his childhood or his early education. Very much later, when his mystical teachings attracted scholars and philosophers throughout China—and even beyond its borders—a great number of legends grew up about him. And these legends, too, were wrapped in cryptic symbolism.

Legend has it that Lao-tze was never young. He was born old. At birth his hair was white and his skin wrinkled, and he had the long white beard of advanced age. Because he had been born in the shadow of a plum tree and because his ear lobes were abnormally long, his mother called him Plum-Tree-Ears. But wherever they went, people called him "the Old Philosopher," Lao-tze.

At an early age, according to legend, he became interested in philosophy and was appointed Archivist of the Imperial Library, in the city of Lo-Yang. Lao-tze remained uncommunicative, seeking neither students nor disciples, seeking neither gain nor honors, immersed in his world of the library full of ancient manuscripts. Yet his opinions on religion and philosophy became known in some way to a large and admiring audience.

When he had grown very old, about ninety years old, he decided to leave the library, and the city and province in which it was located, because he disapproved of the tyrannous behavior of the rulers of the place.

He bought himself a small cart and a black ox, and he drove in the cart toward the border of the Province of Chou. But at the crossing, the border guard, Yin Hsi, recognized him, and would not permit him to pass.

Yin Hsi argued with the old man: "You have always kept to yourself like a hermit and have never written down your teachings. Yet many know them. Now you wish to leave and retire beyond our borders. And your teachings will be forgotten. I will not let you cross the border until you have written down the essentials of your teachings."

So Lao-tze tarried at the border long enough to write down in five thousand Chinese characters—divided into eighty-one short poems—what he called *Tao Teh King*.

Then Lao-tze, according to legend, handed his writings to

Yin Hsi and said: "Here is all I have to teach. Now let me pass."

Yin Hsi took the writings from the old man, and after he had read them he placed them reverently upon the gate-house table. Then he turned to the old sage and begged to be permitted to go along as a servant and disciple.

Lao-tze made room for him in the cart, and Yin Hsi climbed in. The black ox drew the cart through the un-guarded gate and rolled out of sight. And the Old Philosopher and his first disciple were never heard of again. Lao-tze disappeared as completely as if he had never existed. But his little book remained.

3. The Mystifying Little Book

That Lao-tze did exist we conclude from the reports that Confucius met with him face to face. And then there is his extraordinary little book: the *Tao Teh King*, or *Tao Teh Ching*, or whichever way the Chinese scholar wishes to pronounce or translate it.

About the man behind this book few details are known. About his teachings, those who wish to know them can learn a great deal. For Lao-tze's small book of about twenty-five pages has inspired an impressive number of weighty volumes which attempt to explain its meaning.

The very first word in the title, the mysterious word *Tao*, has caused scholars unending difficulty. Some of them translate it as "The Way"; some think it means "The Path"; others believe it means "Reason and Virtue"; and there are still others who state that it means "The Word," in the sense in which it was used by the Apostle John.

The opening sentence in the *Tao Teh King* is translated by James Legge as: "The *Tao* that can be trodden is not the enduring and unchanging *Tao*."

The same sentence translated by the distinguished Sinologist, Major-General G. G. Alexander, reads: "God (the great everlasting infinite First Cause from whom all things in heaven and earth proceed) can neither be defined nor named."

With the same text before them, a number of scholars have made translations of the *Tao Teh King* just as varied as the two examples cited. And we will really never know for certain what Lao-tze intended *Tao* to mean. For very early in his book he tells us about *Tao*: "They who know [what it means] do not tell, and they who tell do not know."

In spite of this warning, many disciples and authors who

later interpreted the metaphysical nature of the *Tao Teh King* developed lengthy commentaries on how each of the eighty-one short poems, of which the book consists, should be understood. Some explanations branched off into beliefs and superstitions only remotely related to the teachings of Taoism. And cults soon grew up which reverted to an early stage of Nature-Worship, in which a host of superstitions clustered around dragons and demons, that were in no way related to the teachings of Lao-tze or the contents of his book. Even the serious and scholarly disciples could not agree among themselves as to the beliefs inherent in the puzzling little book which became the Sacred Scriptures of Taoism.

The man who wrote those scriptures, shadowy in his person from the start, is now hidden behind a series of high walls built by his followers, and his teachings are overlaid with the voluminous wrappings of layer upon layer of interpretation and commentary.

The only way to reach the basic beliefs of Taoism is to slash through the accumulated and bewildering commentaries, and to consider the comprehensible parts of the *Tao Teh King,* leaving the commentaries and myths to the scholars of comparative religion.

Nothing of the personal life of Lao-tze has been handed down to us that might throw light on his teachings. To understand them we must therefore return to his slender and mystifying little book. In it we must search for the basic beliefs he left behind to his followers as a guide to follow, a Road, a Way, a Path of Reason and Virtue, which would give meaning and purpose to their lives.

4. The Tao Teh King

Taoism, it is generally assumed, is a metaphysical system derived from the *Tao Teh King,* traditionally ascribed to Lao-tze. Yet there are many scholars who are convinced that the beliefs of Taoism had their origin in a more distant antiquity. James Legge, who translated the *Tao Teh King* and other texts of Taoism nearly a century ago, states in his Introduction:

For more than a thousand years "the Three Religions" has been a stereotyped phrase in China, meaning what we call Confucianism, Taoism, and Buddhism. The phrase itself simply means "the Three Teachings," or systems of instruction, leaving the subject-matter of each "Teaching" to be learned by inquiry. Of the three, Buddhism is of course the most recent, having been introduced into China only in the first century of our Christian Era. Both the others were indigenous to the country, and are traceable to a much greater antiquity, so that it is a question to which the earlier origin should be assigned. The years of Confucius' life lay between B.C. 551 and 478; but his own acknowledgment that he was "a transmitter and not a maker," and the testimony of his grandson, that "he handed down the doctrines of *Yao* and *Sun* (B.C. 2300), and elegantly displayed the regulations of Wan and Wu (B.C. 1200), taking them as his model," are well known.

Lao-tze's birth is said, in the most likely account of it, to have taken place in the third year of King Ting of the Kau dynasty (B.C. 604). He was thus rather more than fifty years older than Confucius. . . . It is a peculiarity of the *Tao Teh King* that any historical element in it is of the vaguest nature possible, and in all its chapters there is not a single proper name. Yet there are some references to earlier sages whose words the author was copying out, and to "sentence-makers" whose maxims he was introducing to illustrate his own sentiments. In the most distant antiquity he saw a happy society in which his highest ideas of the *Tao* were realized, and in the seventeenth chapter he tells us that in the earliest times the people did not know that there were rulers, and when those rulers were most successful in dealing with them, simply said, "We are what we are of ourselves." Evidently, men existed to Lao-tze at first in a condition of happy innocence—in what he must call a paradisiacal state, according to his idea of what such a state was likely to be.

James Legge (and others before and after him) saw in the *Tao Teh King* a systematized presentation, in the poetic and condensed form peculiar to its time and place, based, in part at least, on ancient and time-honored maxims which pointed the way to a "paradisiacal" state.

But whether the *Tao Teh King* was an original work of an inspired sage, or a creation stimulated by ancient "sentence-makers," it became the sacred scriptures of a new religion, though the religion had little semblance to the teachings of Lao-tze. Nor was its acceptance immediate.

Just as Confucianism was established by Mencius, a disciple who was born nearly a hundred years after the death of Confucius, so Taoism was established by Chuang-tze, a disciple and prolific writer who lived nearly two centuries after the death of Lao-tze.

5. The Disciple Chuang-tze

The Old Philosopher left the legacy of a little book of five thousand Chinese characters. His disciple Chuang-tze wrote fifty-two books, of which thirty-three survive. Chuang-tze's books became very popular in China, and he was greatly admired. Though all his lively books were written to prove the esoteric teachings of his Master and to attack any teachings opposing or rivaling them, Chuang-tze soon became venerated along with Lao-tze. Some even believed that Lao-tze and his work was the invention of Chuang-tze, and were used to illustrate whatever point he wished to make.

Chuang-tze used exaggeration and lively fantasy to illustrate Lao-tze's teachings. His humor is evident in the following taken from his story "Enjoyment in Untroubled Ease":

In the bare and barren north there is the dark and vast ocean—the Pool of Heaven. In it there is a bird named the *phang;* its back is like the Thai mountain, while its wings are like clouds all round the sky. On a whirlwind it mounts upward as on the whorls of a goat's horn for 90,000 li, till, far removed from the cloudy vapors, it bears on its back the blue sky, and then it shapes its course for the South, and proceeds to the ocean there.

A quail by the side of a marsh laughed at it, and said, "Where is it going to? I spring up with a bound, and come down again when I have reached but a few fathoms, and then fly about among the brushwood and bushes; and this is the perfection of flying. Where is that creature going to?"

This shows the difference between the small and the great.

After Chuang-tze other writers and interpreters arose; and Taoism became established as a religion. But it quickly deteriorated into a tangle of irrelevant superstitions, magic and divination. In time Lao-tze was deified. And when Buddhism reached China and became established there, Taoism borrowed from Buddhism the concept of reincarnation, believing that Lao-tze was a reincarnation of the Buddha. Shrines arose; in Taoist temples orders of monks appeared. And a great number of rites and charms were practiced that had no connection with the teachings of Lao-tze, which are preserved in a group of lofty ethical concepts.

For nearly a thousand years Taoism rivaled Confucianism and influenced every aspect of Chinese culture. Taoism early divided into two movements: one purely philosophic and the other, religious.

As a philosophy, its basic was Naturalism, in which the role of the Mother in the scheme of things was extolled. Simplicity was the key to knowledge, as patience was to understanding. Compassion and kindness were keys to friendship. And tranquillity was the assurance of the good life.

As a religion Taoism deteriorated into a search for longevity, a delving into magic ways of restoring youth, and into diverse superstitious practices which were believed to lead to earthly immortality. The followers of Taoism reverted to the worship of nature gods. They began to worship Lao-tze as a god, alongside the many gods they had borrowed from Buddhism. And from there they went on to establish a god for everything in existence or in their fertile imagination.

Slowly Taoism and Buddhism exerted such an influence upon each other that it became difficult to tell them apart in their rituals and their ceremonies. But as the influence of Confucianism increased, Taoism began to decline. Yet the influence of Lao-tze, not as a god or a religious leader, but as a great mystic and ethical teacher, continued in China. And the memory of the Old Philosopher never dimmed because of the inheritance he left to his people in the *Tao Teh King*.

6. What Taoism Believes

The basic beliefs and doctrines of Taoism are to be found in the *Tao Teh King*. There are many translations and interpretations of this slender sheaf of epigrammatic poems. For to each reflective person they can be made to yield a meaning in a different way. The difficulties of translating the classic Chinese of this book are great enough, and many translators have added the additional difficulty of attempting to render Chinese poetry into English poetry.

The translation by Professor James Legge gives a suggestion of the poetic form of the original, although the major part is given in prose.

7. Chapters from the Tao Teh King

● CHAPTER I: THE TAO THAT CAN BE TRODDEN

The Tao that can be trodden is not the enduring and unchanging Tao. The name that can be named is not the enduring and unchanging name.

Conceived of as having no name, it is the Originator of heaven and earth· conceived of a having a name, it is the Mother of all things.

> Always without desire we must be found,
> If its deep mystery we would sound;
> But if desire always within us be,
> Its outer fringe is all that we shall see.

Under these two aspects, it is really the same; but as development takes place, it receives the different names. Together we call them the Mystery. Where the Mystery is the deepest is the gate of all that is subtle and wonderful.

● CHAPTER II: ALL IN THE WORLD KNOW

All in the world know the beauty of the beautiful, and in doing this they have the idea of what ugliness is; they all know the skill of the skillful, and in doing this they have the idea of what the want of skill is.

So it is that existence and non-existence give birth the one to the idea of the other;

That difficulty and ease produce the one the idea of the other;

That length and shortness fashion out the one the figure of the other;

That the ideas of height and lowness arise from the contrast of the one with the other;

That the musical notes and tones become harmonious through the relation of one with another; and

That being before and behind give the idea of one following another.

Therefore the sage manages affairs without doing anying, and conveys his instructions without the use of speech.

All things spring up, and there is not one which declines to show itself; they grow, and there is no claim made for their ownership; they go through their processes, and there is no expectation of a reward for the results. The work is accomplished, and there is no resting in it as an achievement.

> The work is done, but how no one can see;
> 'Tis this that makes the power not cease to be.

● CHAPTER XI: THE THIRTY SPOKES

The thirty spokes unite in the one nave; but it is on the empty space for the axle, that the use of the wheel depends.

Clay is fashioned into vessels; but it is on their empty hollowness, that their use depends. The door and windows are cut out from the walls to form an apartment; but it is on the empty space within, that its use depends. Therefore, what has a positive existence serves for profitable adaptation, and what has not that for actual usefulness.

● CHAPTER XIV: WE LOOK AT IT

We look at it, and we do not see it, and we name it "the Equable."

We listen to it, and we do not hear it, and we name it "the Inaudible."

We try to grasp it, and do not get hold of it, and we name it "the Subtle."

With these three qualities, it can not be made the subject of description; and hence we blend them together and obtain The One.

Its upper part is not bright, and its lower part is not obscure.

Ceaseless in its action, it yet can not be named, and then it again returns and becomes nothing. This is called the Form of the Formless, and the Semblance of the Invisible; this is called the Fleeting and the Indeterminable.

We meet it and do not see its Front;

We follow it, and do not see its Back.

When we can lay hold of the Tao of old to direct the things of the present day, and are able to know it as it was of old in the beginning, this is called unwinding the clue of Tao.

● CHAPTER XXI: THE GRANDEST FORMS

> The grandest forms of active force
> From Tao come, their only source.
> Who can of Tao the nature tell?
> Our sight it flies, our touch as well.
> Eluding sight, eluding touch,
> The forms of things all in it crouch;
> Eluding touch, eluding sight,
> There are their semblances, all right.
> Profound it is, dark and obscure;
> Things' essences all there endure.
> Those essences the truth enfold
> Of what, when seen, shall then be told.
> Now it is so; 'twas so of old.
> Its name—what passes not away;

> So, in their beautiful array,
> Things form and never know decay.

How know I that it is so with all the beauties of existing things? By this nature of the Tao.

● CHAPTER XXIV: HE WHO STANDS

He who stands on his tiptoes does not stand firm;
He who stretches his legs does not walk easily.
So, he who displays himself does not shine;
He who asserts his own views is not distinguished;
He who vaunts himself does not find his merit acknowledged;
He who is self-conceited has no superiority allowed to him.
Such conditions, viewed from the standpoint of the Tao, are like remnants of food, or a tumor on the body, which all dislike.
Hence those who pursue the course of the Tao do not adopt and allow them.

● CHAPTER XXV: THERE WAS SOMETHING

There was something undefined and complete, coming into existence before Heaven and Earth. How still it was and formless, standing alone, and undergoing no change, reaching everywhere and in no danger of being exhausted! It may be regarded as the Mother of all things.
I do not know its name, and I give it the designation of the Tao (the Way or Course). Making an effort further to give it a name I call it The Great.
Great, it passes on in constant flow. Passing on, it becomes remote. Having become remote, it returns. Therefore the Tao is great; Heaven is great; Earth is great; and the sage king is also great. In the universe there are four that are great, and the sage king is one of them.
Man takes his law from the Earth; the Earth takes its law from Heaven; Heaven takes its law from the Tao. The law of the Tao is its being what it is.

● CHAPTER XXXIII: HE WHO KNOWS

He who knows other men is discerning; he who knows himself is intelligent.
He who overcomes others is strong; he who overcomes himself is mighty.

He who is satisfied with his lot is rich; he who goes on acting with energy has a firm will.

He who does not fail in the requirements of his position continues long; he who dies and yet does not perish has longevity.

● CHAPTER XLVII: WITHOUT GOING OUTSIDE

Without going outside his door, one understands all that takes place under the sky;

Without looking out from the window, one sees the Tao of Heaven.

The farther that one goes out from himself, the less he knows.

Therefore the sages got their knowledge without traveling; gave their right names to things without seeing them; and accomplished their ends without any purpose of doing so.

● CHAPTER XLIX: THE SAGE

The sage has no invariable mind of his own; he makes the mind of the people his mind.

To those who are good to me, I am good; and to those who are not good to me, I am also good—and thus all get to be good.

To those who are sincere with me, I am sincere; and to those who are not sincere with me, I am also sincere—and thus all get to be sincere.

The sage has in the world an appearance of indecision, and keeps his mind in a state of indifference to all. The people all keep their eyes and ears directed to him, and he deals with them all as his children.

● CHAPTER LI: ALL THINGS

All things are produced by the Tao, and nourished by its outflowing operation.

They receive their forms according to the nature of each, and are completed according to the circumstances of their condition.

Therefore all things without exception honor the Tao, and exalt its outflowing operation.

This honoring of the Tao and exalting of its operation are not the result of any ordination, but always a spontaneous tribute.

Thus it is that the Tao produces all things, nourishes them, brings them to their full growth, nurses them, completes them, matures them, maintains them, and overspreads them.

It produces them and makes no claim to the possession of them;

It carries them through their processes and does not vaunt its ability in doing so;

It brings them to maturity and exercises no control over them;

This is called its mysterious operation.

CHAPTER LIV: TAO'S SKILLFUL PLANTER

What Tao's skillful planter plants
 Can never be uptorn;
What his skillful arms enfold,
 From him can ne'er be borne.
 Sons shall bring in lengthening line
 Sacrifices to his shrine.
 Tao when nursed within one's self,
 His vigor will make true;
And where the family it rules,
 What riches will accrue!
The neighborhood where it prevails
 No thieving will abound;
And when 'tis seen throughout the State,
 Good fortune will be found.
Employ it the kingdom o'er,
 And men thrive all around.

In this way the effect will be seen in the person, by the observation of different cases; in the family; in the neighborhood; in the State; and in the kingdom.

How do I know that this effect is sure to hold thus all under the sky? By this method of observation.

CHAPTER LVI: HE WHO KNOWS THE TAO

He who knows the Tao does not care to speak about it; he who is ever ready to speak about it does not know it.

He who knows it will keep his mouth shut and close the portals of his nostrils. He will blunt his sharp points and unravel the complications of things; he will attemper his brightness, and bring himself into agreement with the obscurity of others. This is called "the Mysterious Agreement."

Such a one can not be treated familiarly or distantly; he

is beyond all consideration of profit or injury; of nobility or meanness—he is the noblest man under heaven.

● CHAPTER LXIII: IT IS THE WAY

It is the way of the Tao to act without thinking of acting;
To conduct affairs without feeling the trouble of them;
To taste without discerning any flavor;
To consider what is small as great, and a few as many; and
To recompense injury with kindness.
The master of it anticipates things that are difficult while they are easy, and does things that would become great while they are small.
All difficult things in the world are sure to arise from a previous state in which they were easy, and all great things from one in which they were small. Therefore the sage, while he never does what is great, is able on that account to accomplish the greatest things.
He who lightly promises is sure to keep but little faith; He who is continually thinking things easy is sure to find them difficult. Therefore the sage sees difficulty even in what seems easy, and so never has any difficulties.

● CHAPTER LXVIII: IN TAO'S WARS

He who in Tao's wars has skill
    Assumes no martial port;
He who fights with most good will
    To rage makes no resort.
He who vanquishes yet still
    Keeps from his foes apart;
He whose hests men most fulfill
    Yet humbly plies his art.

Thus we say, "He ne'er contends,
    And therein is his might."
Thus we say, "Men's wills he bends,
    That they with him unite."
Thus we say, "Like Heaven's his ends,
    No sage of old more bright."

● CHAPTER LXXVII: MAY NOT TAO BE COMPARED?

May not the Way (or Tao) of Heaven be compared to the method of bending a bow? The part of the bow which was high is brought low, and what was low is raised up.

So Heaven diminishes where there is superabundance, and supplements where there is deficiency.

It is the Way of Heaven to diminish superabundance, and to supplement deficiency. It is not so with the way of man. He takes away from those who have not enough to add to his own superabundance.

Who can take his own superabundance and therewith serve all under heaven? Only he who is in possession of the Tao!

Therefore the ruling sage acts without claiming the results as his; he achieves his merit and does not rest arrogantly in it—he does not wish to display his superiority.

- CHAPTER LXXXI: SINCERE WORDS

Sincere words are not fine; fine words are not sincere.

Those who are skilled in the Tao do not dispute about it; the disputatious are not skilled in it.

Those who know the Tao are not extensively learned; the extensively learned do not know it.

The sage does not accumulate for himself. The more he expends for others, the more does he possess of his own; the more that he gives to others, the more does he have himself.

With all the sharpness of the Way of Heaven, it injures not; with all the doing in the way of the sage, he does not strive.

The last chapter of the *Tao Teh King*, Chapter LXXXI, is called "The Manifestation of Simplicity." This is considered to show how the Tao proceeds, quietly and effectively, and by contraries, in a way only the master of it can understand. And, according to Wu Chang, Lao-tze "sums up in this the subject-matter of the two parts of his Treatise, showing that in all its five thousand characters there is nothing beyond what is here said."

8. Sayings from the Tao Teh King

Nameless are the origins of all creation.

Those who are motivated by desire see only the outer shell of things.

Good implies the idea of evil; and beauty implies the idea of ugliness.

The wise man does not teach by words but by deeds.

The Way is like an empty vessel which is the ancestry from which come all things in the world.

The excellence of a government is judged by its order.

The value of an act is judged by its timing.

Thirty spokes unite in the hub, but the worth of the wheel will depend on the void where the axle turns.

What gives a clay cup value is the empty space its walls create.

Usefulness is to be found in non-existence.

The five colors will blind the eye; the five sounds will deafen the ear; the five flavors will weary the taste; things hard to get will do harm to man's conduct. Therefore the wise will provide for the heart and not for the eye.

If you know righteousness, though you die, you shall not perish.

If you trust people not enough, they may trust you not at all.

Get rid of your preachers and discard your teachers, and the people will benefit a hundredfold. Root out your schemers and renounce your profiteers, and thieving will disappear.

Between "yes" and "no" how small the difference; between "good" and "evil" how great the difference.

He who humbles himself shall be preserved; he who bends shall be made straight; he who is empty shall be filled; and he who has little shall succeed.

He who is not a competitor, no one in the whole world can compete with him.

If you work by the Way, you will be of the Way.

Little faith is put in those who have little faith.

There is something that existed before the earth and the sky began and its name is the Way.

Man conforms to the earth; the earth conforms to the sky; the sky conforms to the Way; the Way conforms to its own nature.

Observe all the white around you, but remember all the black that is there.

As for those who would take the whole world to tinker with as they see fit, observe that they never succeed.

The wise reject all extremes.

Where troops march, there thorns will spring up; and where armies are gathered, there famine will enter.

Weapons of war are tools of evil; those who truly admire them are murderers at heart.

Those who are on the Way might be compared to rivulets flowing into the sea.

He who understands others is wise; he who understands himself is enlightened.

He who conquers others is strong; he who conquers his own will is mighty.

The great Form is without form; it is nothing to see and nothing to hear, yet it is timeless and endures.

If you would take, you must first give, this is the beginning of intelligence.

Absence of desires brings tranquillity.

True compassion is known by its good deeds.

A cart is more than the sum of its parts.

The great Space has no corners; the great Form has no shape.

The Way is nameless and hidden, yet all things gain their fulfillment in it.

The best instruction is not in words.

Perfection is an imperfection.

Activity overcomes cold; inactivity overcomes heat: so the wise man by his calm sets everything right in the world.

Where the Way rules, horses are bred for farms; where the Way does not rule, horses are bred for armies.

Without leaving the house one may know the entire world; without looking out of the window, one may see the heavens.

The world is lost to those who try to win it.

To the good I would be good, and to the bad I would be good; in that way all might become good.

If you see what is small, you have clearness of vision; if you store up small energies, you gain strength.

The wise man is moved neither by affection nor hatred, by profit nor loss, by honor nor shame. And for that reason he is held in high esteem by the entire world.

Wars are best waged by stratagem; but people are best governed by forthrightness.

The more prohibitions, the more poverty; the more laws, the more crimes; the more skills, the more luxuries; the more weapons, the more chaos.

In serving Heaven and in ruling men use moderation.

Govern a large country as you would fry a small fish (without overdoing it).

Was it not said that the seeker will find the Way, and the sinner who finds it will be forgiven?

Everything difficult must be dealt with while it is still easy.

A thousand-mile journey can be made one step at a time.

Three things prize above all: gentleness, frugality and humility. For the gentle can be bold, the frugal can be liberal and the humble can become leaders of men.

If you cannot advance an inch, retreat a foot.

The wise man wears a coarse garment, but carries a jewel in his bosom.

To know that one does not know, that is healthy. To think one knows what he does not know, that is a disease. Not in words does God get answers.

Everyone knows the paradox that the weak will overcome the strong, and the gentle will prevail in the end.

The Way of heaven is impartial; but it favors good men.

The ideal land is small, its people few, its tools ten times or even a hundred times beyond their needs. There people live and die and never emigrate. They have weapons and armor that are never used and never displayed. Their food is sweet; their clothes adorned; their homes are at peace, and their customs full of charm. The neighboring lands are so close that each may hear the other's crowing cocks and barking dogs. Yet men grow old and never once exchange a contentious call.

7   SHINTO

Kami-no-Michi

1. Land of the Rising Sun

China is the land of Three Teachings: Confucianism, Taoism, and Buddhism. Two are native, and one originated in India. Japan also is a land of Three Teachings: Confucianism, Buddhism, and Shinto. One is native, one came from China and one from India. But the native teaching, Shinto, has so influenced and colored the other two that they merged and blended to suit the character of this Island people, and their, until recently, insular way of life.

Why Shinto remains an insular and national religion, wedded to its place of origin, becomes clearer when we know how it arose.

At a very early period, recorded only in myth and sacred folklore, the Japanese believed that they were the only people on earth. They lived on the Great-Eight-Island-Land, surrounded by thousands of small uninhabited islands. Beyond them, and all about them, were the waters of the great ocean that covered the rest of the flat earth. Heaven was not too far above. And a floating bridge connected heaven and earth. Underneath the earth was the underworld which could be reached by anyone who wished to go down there. Heaven was populated by people and all the living things that are on earth, excepting that they were much finer and more beautiful. And the Underworld, too, was full of beings similar to those on earth, excepting they were not as nice.

Then a great earthquake destroyed the Bridge to Heaven and blocked the entrance to the Underworld with a great stone. Ever since that time men could neither go up to visit Heaven nor go down to see the people in the Underworld.

Another ancient legend * relates that one day two gods (of whom there were many in Heaven) decided to visit the water-covered earth. These two, Izanagi and his younger sister Izanami, took the Heavenly Jeweled Spear and, standing upon the Bridge of Heaven, churned the briny waters with their gleaming weapon. When they lifted the spear, large drops of briny water dripped down from its end; and where they fell, there the island Onogoso appeared.

To this island the two gods, who were of the Seventh Generation of Gods, went down to live upon it. And Izanagi said to his younger sister:

"Let us go around the Heavenly Pillar, and when we meet on the other side let us unite and create children."

So Izanagi went to the right and Izanami went to the left, and when they met on the other side, she exclaimed:

"Oh, what a sublime and lovable youth you are, Izanagi!"

And he replied: "Oh, what a sublime and lovable maiden you are, Izanami!"

From their union an island was born, and they named it *Futa-na*. Afterwards many other islands were born to them, which they named. The birth of Deities followed. And later came the birth of Three Illustrious Children: the Sun-Goddess, the Moon-God, and the Storm-God.

The Sun-Goddess, Izanagi's favorite, he named *Amaterasu-omi-Kami*, and she gave him no trouble whatsoever. But the Storm-God, *Susa-no-Wo*, was a rebellious son, and Izanagi finally expelled him from the land.

After many adventures with the impetuous *Susa-no-Wo*, *Amaterasu-omi-Kami* also had a family; and her grandson, *Jimmu Tenno*, became the first Emperor, or Mikado, of Japan.

And that is the description given in the earliest records of how the Land of the Rising Sun came into being.

* Given in the *Kojiki*, the oldest of the Shinto sacred scriptures.

2. The Way of the Gods

When and from where the aborigines of Japan invaded the islands we do not know. Credible guesses have been made that they came from northern Asia via Korea, over a number of centuries before the Christian Era.

At that remote period in the past the Japanese were a primitive aggregate of different kinds of people, who had no written language. Their religion was simple nature-worship, with the skies above inhabited by many manlike gods, early divided into opposed yet complementary male and female spirits.

At an early date the Japanese had no name for their religion, and nowhere in their earliest legends is the word "religion" used. When they assembled what was to become the first of their Sacred Scriptures, in A.D. 712, they called it "Records of Ancient Things" (*Kojiki*), in which was related the history of their first Emperor, and his antecedents among the manlike gods in heaven.

When the Japanese people came in contact with the Chinese they adopted Chinese writing, Chinese Buddhism and Confucianism, and many other cultural elements of China. Yet they so adapted the Chinese religions and invested them with their own primitive rituals and beliefs, that they emerged as a native faith, which the Chinese called: the Way of the Gods, or *Shin-tao*. And it has been known by its Chinese name, Shinto, ever since, although the name in Japanese is *Kami-no-Michi*.

3. The Beautiful and the Divine

Unlike the other living religions, with the exception of Judaism, Shinto is part of a history. A Shintoist, as a Japanese, had to be, until recently, unqualifiably loyal to the Emperor as a descendant of the Sun-Goddess.

An outstanding authority on Shinto, D. C. Holton, writes:

Into this religion [Shinto] the Japanese individual is born; loyalty to its belief and practice is his first qualification as a "good Japanese." It is not his by election; even when he chooses to attach himself to a universal religion like Buddhism or Christianity, the old is ever there as a vital, all-pervading influence, fundamentally conditioning his mentality

and conduct and supplying a pattern to which all else must
be accommodated.

Through many generations Shinto has inculcated a profound love of nature, which is deeply rooted in the Land
of the Rising Sun. The very stones and flowers, the trees
and streams of Japan are associated with rituals and prayers
that have a special meaning to the Shintoist. Even the
houses about him are built with a particular relation to the
sun. For the adoration of the rising sun has been followed
traditionally ever since *Jimmu Tenno* ascended the throne
and became the first emperor in 660 B.C.—which is the first
year in the Japanese era.

Shintoists have many temples to which they go for prayer.
There are no idols and no images in them. The offerings
brought by the people are mirrors or food or spears; and
their prayers are for immediate needs.

Young and old wake early when they can to greet the
sunrise and to admire the dawn. Sunrise is a favorite theme
in Japanese poetry, which has become noted for its brevity
and beauty. But their admiration does not extend to the
sunset, which Japanese consider a sad time of the day. They
express their religious adoration of *Amaterasu-omi-Kami* in
their reverence for the sunrise, as well as for all things that
grow or flow: flowers, forests, streams and rivers. These are
the preferred subjects of paintings, they are the themes in
songs, and there are many prayers to them. And through
their worship of nature they have developed a love of art
and a love of sunlit beauty to the degree that beauty has
become part of their religion.

And beauty, to the Shintoist, is not something about
which merely to contemplate; beauty is something to be
experienced in every day of living. For to the Shintoist the
beautiful in nature is the Divine.

4. Three Shinto Prayers

In the *Yengishiki,* we find the following prayers, which
show the intermingling of religious feelings and the feeling
for nature:

● THE HARVEST RITUAL

I declare in the presence of the sovereign gods of the
Harvest,

If the sovereign gods will bestow, in many-bundled spikes and in luxuriant spikes,

The late-ripening harvest which they will bestow,

The late-ripening harvest which will be produced by the dripping of foam from the arms, and by drawing the mud together between the opposing thighs,

Then I will fulfill their praises by presenting the first-fruits in a thousand ears and in many hundred ears;

Raising high the beer-jars, filling and ranging in rows the bellies of the beer-jars,

I will present them in juice and in grain.

As to things which grow in the great field plain—sweet herbs and bitter herbs;

As to things which dwell in the blue sea plain—things wide of fin, and things narrow of fin, down to the weeds of the offing, and weeds of the shore;

And as to clothes, with bright cloth, glittering cloth, soft cloth, and coarse cloth will I fulfill their praises.

And having furnished a white horse, a white boar, and a white cock,

And the various kinds of things in the presence of the sovereign gods of the Harvest, I fulfill their praises by presenting the great Offerings of the sovereign Grandchild's augustness.

● RITUALS TO THE SUN-GODDESS: II

I declare in the great presence of the From-Heaven-shining-great-deity who sits in Ise.

Because the Sovereign great goddess bestows on him the countries of the four quarters over which her glance extends,

As far as the limit where Heaven stands up like a wall,

As far as the bounds where the country stands up distant,

As far as the limit where the blue clouds spread flat,

As far as the bounds where the white clouds lie away fallen—

The blue sea plain as far as the limit whither come the prows of the ships without drying poles or paddles,

The ships which continuously crowd on the great sea plain,

And the roads which men travel by land, as far as the limit whither come the horses' hoofs, with the baggage-cords tied tightly, treading the uneven rocks and tree-roots and standing up continuously in a long path without a break—

Making the narrow countries wide and the hilly countries plain,

And as it were drawing together the distant countries by throwing many tens of ropes over them—

He will pile up the first-fruits like a range of hills in the great presence of the Sovereign great goddess, and will peacefully enjoy the remainder.

● THE PURIFICATION RITUAL

Amongst the various sorts of offenses which may be committed in ignorance or out of negligence by Heaven's increasing people,

Who shall come into being in the country, which the Sovereign Grandchild's augustness, hiding in the fresh residence,

Built by stoutly planting the house-pillars on the bottommost rocks,

And exalting the cross-beams to the plain of high Heaven, as his shade from the Heavens and shade from the sun, shall tranquilly rule as a peaceful country, namely, the country of great Yamato,

Where the sun is seen on high, which he fixed upon as a peaceful country, as the center of the countries of the four quarters thus bestowed upon him—

Breaking the ridges, filling up watercourses, opening sluices, doubly sowing, planting stakes, flaying alive, flaying backward, and dunging;

Many of such offenses are distinguished as Heavenly offenses, and as earthly offenses;

Cutting living flesh, cutting dead flesh, leprosy, proud flesh, the offense committed with one's own mother, the offense committed with one's own child, the offense committed with mother and child, the offense committed with child and mother, the offense committed with beasts, calamities of crawling worms, calamities of a god on high, calamities of birds on high, the offenses of killing beasts and using incantations;

Many of such offenses may be disclosed.

When he has, thus repeated it, the Heavenly gods will push open Heaven's eternal gates,

And cleaving a path with might through the manifold clouds of Heaven, will hear;

And the country gods, ascending to the tops of the high mountains, and to the tops of the low hills, and tearing asunder the mists of the high mountains, and the mists of the low hills, will hear.

And when they have thus heard, the Maiden-of-Descent-into-the-Current, who dwells in the current of the swift stream which boils down the ravines from the tops of the high mountains, and the tops of the low hills,

Shall carry out to the great sea plain the offenses which are cleared away and purified, so that there be no remaining offense;

Like as Shinato's wind blows apart the manifold clouds of Heaven,

As the morning wind and the evening wind blow away the morning mist and the evening mist,

As the great ships which lie on the shore of the great port loosen their prows, and loosen their sterns to push out into the great sea plain;

As the trunks of the forest trees, far and near, are cleared away by the sharp sickle, the sickle forged with fire;

So that there cease to be any offense called an offense in the court of the Sovereign Grandchild's augustness to begin with, and in the countries of the four quarters of the region under Heaven.

And when she thus carries them out and away, the deity called the Maiden-of-the-Swift-Cleansing, who dwells in the multitudinous meetings of the sea-waters, the multitudinous currents of rough sea-waters shall gulp them down.

And when she has thus gulped them down, the lord of the Breath-blowing-place, who dwells in the Breath-blowing-place, shall utterly blow them away with his breath to the Root-country, the Bottom-country.

And when he has thus blown them away, the deity called the Maiden-of-Swift-Banishment, who dwells in the Root-country, the Bottom-country, shall completely banish them, and get rid of them.

And when they have thus been got rid of, there shall from this day onward be no offense which is called offense, with regard to the men of the offices who serve in the court of the Sovereign, nor in the four quarters of the region under Heaven.

[Then the high priest says:]

Hear all of you how he leads forth the horse as a thing that erects its ears toward the plain of high Heaven, and deigns to sweep away and purify with the general purification, as the evening sun goes down on the last day of the watery moon of this year.

O diviners of the four countries, take the sacrifices away out of the river highway, and sweep them away.

5. What Shinto Believes

To explain the elusive Shinto approach, the Japanese commentator, Inazo Nitobe, puts it this way:

A "Naturefolk" learns by intimate contact with nature that there is a healing power in the flower and the grass, in the mountains and streams, in the rain and the clouds. He comes to see gods working in these phenomena, and if they are of divine origin, do they not contain goodly qualities? Why seek afar for the divine? It is even in the objects around you. They are good and just. Why seek elsewhere for justice and goodness? So, to live a natural life is to be just and good. There is no evil in nature. What seems to be evil is the tipping of the balance scale. Evil is immoderation. All natural appetites are good and they become evil only when indulged in to excess. This is Shinto, the Way of the Gods, naïve primitive teaching aboriginal to the soil of Japan.

Though, of course, the Japanese have a code of ethics; beliefs in the life hereafter, and concepts of sin and penance; these they acquired when they accepted Buddhism. In their native Shintoist beliefs they condemn theft and lying; adultery and incest, and bestiality and witchcraft; though they have no revealed commandments against them.

Their code of behavior is the Code of the Knight, or the Code of the Noble. And this Code begins with:

Courage. The first virtue in the Shinto code is courage, and it is taught to children as early as they can understand it. When a child hurts himself and begins to cry, the parents reprimand him for succumbing to such a weakness because of a little pain. And when a boy reaches the age of seven or eight, his father asks: "Would you die for your father?" And if the answer, "I would," is not made immediately, the boy is punished. Their attitude toward courage is epitomized in the saying: "It is true courage to live when it is right to live, and to die when it is right to die."

Cowardice. Just as courage in every form is extolled, cowardice is condemned as a sin. This is made quite clear in their saying: "All sins, great and small, may be forgiven by repentance, except two: cowardice and theft."

Loyalty. Next to courage, or even preceding it, comes the virtue of loyalty. Until recently the first loyalty belonged to the Emperor. Then it extended to members within the family, to the community, and also to future generations.

Cleanliness. In the Shinto ritual cleanliness has an important place. Much time is devoted to purification. To be unclean is a sin. For uncleanliness is an offense to the gods. And the consideration of what might be displeasing to the gods gave rise to a large body of rituals and observances, all having the same objective—not to offend or show disrespect to them.

As an outgrowth of this approach, bathing in Japan is both a purification and a religious rite. The bathroom is an inviting place, and the hours of bathing are set by tradition as the two hours in the afternoon, between five and seven, before the evening meal. There are fixed ceremonies, and even holidays, devoted to bathing.

Today the many Shintoist sects are almost, although not quite, as diverse as the Christian sects. But all of them adhere to the basic tenets that teach them:

To be courageous, loyal, and to observe cleanliness;

That the Father and Mother of the Japanese race stem from Izanagi and Izanami;

That Life is good;

That the world reveals itself in beauty—particularly in dignity and simplicity; and

That deeds are more important than arguments. They express it in the saying: "The hand is mightier than the mouth."

Among the sects that have evolved formal Decalogues are two, the *Shinri Kyo* and *Shinshu Kyo*.

6. Ten Precepts of Shinri Kyo

1. Do not transgress the will of the gods.
2. Do not forget your obligations to ancestors.
3. Do not transgress the decrees of the State.
4. Do not forget the profound goodness of the gods whereby misfortune is averted and sickness is healed.
5. Do not forget that the world is one great family.
6. Do not forget the limitations of your own person.
7. Even though others become angry, do not become angry yourself.
8. Do not be slothful in your business.
9. Do not be a person who brings blame to the teaching.
10. Do not be carried away by foreign teaching.

7. Ten Precepts of Shinshu Kyo

1. Worship the great deities of this sect.
2. Pacify thy spirit, for it is part of the spirit of deity.
3. Practice the Way of the Gods.
4. Revere the divine origin of the State.
5. Be loyal to the ruler.
6. Be zealous in filial piety toward thy parents.
7. Be kind to others.
8. Be diligent in business.
9. Preserve steadfastness within thy breast.
10. Cleanse away the rust of thy body.

Although the attempt has been made in this brief presentation to isolate Shinto, this can no longer be done, for, as stated at the outset, it has absorbed elements and beliefs from Confucianism and, to an even greater extent, from Buddhism. At this time we can catch only glimpses of this early religion as it may have been in its pure and original form.

8. Shinto Sayings

Both heaven and hell come from one's own heart.

All men are brothers; all receive the blessings of the same heaven.

With God there is neither day nor night, neither far nor near.

Faith is just like filial obedience to parents.

When prayer fails to help you accomplish your purpose, know that something is lacking in your sincerity.

Do not profess love with your lips while you harbor hatred in your heart.

One should not be mindful of suffering in his own life and unmindful of suffering in the lives of others.

Happy is the man who cultivates the things that are hidden and lets the things that are apparent take care of themselves.

When the heart of *Amaterasu-omi-Kami* and our hearts are undivided, then there is no such thing as death.

In all the world there is no such thing as a stranger.

8 JUDAISM

Religion of the Prophets

1. "Hear, O Israel—"

Among the living religions Judaism presents a strange paradox. Although it gave birth to two religions, Christianity and Islam, whose followers now comprise over one-half of the world's population, the following of Judaism itself has remained small throughout the centuries.

The limited growth of Judaism can be traced to the history of its early beginnings. For Judaism, from the start, evolved not only as a religion, but as a way of life in a land that itself became identified with the religion; and the language of the land, Hebrew, also became identified with Judaism. While the beliefs of Judaism are those of a universal religion, its history has associated it with a national group, speaking a national language in their native land.

Like most religions whose beginnings go back many centuries before the Christian Era, Judaism, one of the oldest among the living religions, had its origin in a past so dim and distant that we can only speculate about it. It is recorded as beginning about four thousand years ago with a Chaldean named Abram, or Abraham.

The little we know about Abraham is told in the Bible and in extra-Biblical stories that grew up about him. Abraham was born in the city of Ur in the Chaldees, where a great civilization flourished and where a highly developed religion existed which was a merger of Sumerian and Babylonian beliefs. By the time of Abraham's birth, the Chaldeans had a codified set of laws consonant with their beliefs; a complex ritual suited to their times, their temperament and their tradition. They had, too, an oral and written mythology which contained the then-accepted explanation of how and when the world was created; how man was given dominion over the earth and everything upon it; and how man was kept accountable to the Creators—of whom there were many.

Abraham may have accepted most of the beliefs, the rituals, and the myths of his ancestors. But there was one belief he could not accept. This was the belief in many gods,

each supreme in his own sphere. In the Chaldees there
were gods of the sky and the earth, gods of fire and water
and all the natural elements, gods of rainfall and storms, and
numerous lesser gods. Supplementing the gods of natural
phenomena were the city gods—a god for every city in the
land.

When the Chaldeans wanted to pay homage to their gods,
they made images, large and small, to represent them. And
these they worshiped. By the time Abraham was a young
man, the worship of idols had become established in his native land.

Just what induced Abraham to revolt against idol-worship,
and how this led him to the idea that there could not be many
gods but only One—creator and ruler of all that exists on
earth and in heaven—that we will never know. In the story
of Abraham as it is told in the Bible, no mention is made
of Abraham's revolt against idol-worship. The saga of Abraham begins in this way:

Now the Lord said to Abram (Abraham), "Go forth from
your country and your kindred and your father's house to
the land that I will show you. And I will make you a great
nation, and I will bless you, and make your name great so
that you will be a blessing."

After that God reveals Himself to Abraham many times.
Sometimes, we are told, God "came to Abraham in a vision,"
and sometimes God spoke to Abraham through an "angel of
the Lord." And we are told that once, "When the sun was
going down, a deep sleep fell on Abraham; and, lo, a dread,
even a great darkness fell upon him." In that deep dark sleep
the Lord revealed to Abraham that his descendants would be
slaves in Egypt for four hundred years before they would be
delivered and brought to the Promised Land.

When Abraham was very old, God appeared to him to
make a Covenant that was to be kept by all Abraham's
descendants throughout the generations. With this "Everlasting Covenant" God promised Abraham's descendants
"all the land of Canaan for an everlasting possession; and
I will be their God." This Covenant between them was
sanctified in the ancient rite of circumcision, which is kept
by Abraham's descendants to the present day.

The followers of Judaism still identify themselves as "the
Sons of the Covenant" (in Hebrew: B'nai B'rith); and in
their daily prayers they refer to Abraham as "Father Abraham," whom they consider to be the first man to renounce
idolatry; the first man to recognize the existence of One God;

and the first progenitor of the Jewish people—at that time called Hebrews.

Though Abraham's belief in a universal God may differ from the term as it is understood today, his original belief in One God, refined and revised during the passing of the centuries, became the first unquestioned article of faith of Judaism.

2. The Ten Commandments

Some four hundred Biblical years after Abraham, one of his descendants, named Moses, arose and emancipated the Hebrews from their foretold slavery in Egypt, fortified their belief in One God, and strengthened the Covenant Abraham had made with God. Though there is no one founder of Judaism, it was established more concretely by Moses than by any other individual in the long history of this religion. Moses, after freeing his people from slavery, led them to the foot of Mount Sinai, where he brought them two tablets on which were inscribed:

1. I AM THE LORD YOUR GOD, who brought you out of the land of Egypt, out of the house of bondage. You shall have no other gods besides me.
2. YOU SHALL NOT MAKE ANY IMAGE or any manner of likeness of anything that is in heaven above, or on earth below, or that is in the water under the earth.
3. YOU SHALL NOT TAKE THE NAME OF THE LORD IN VAIN.
4. REMEMBER THE SABBATH DAY, to keep it holy.
5. HONOR YOUR FATHER AND YOUR MOTHER.
6. YOU SHALL NOT COMMIT MURDER.
7. YOU SHALL NOT COMMIT ADULTERY.
8. YOU SHALL NOT STEAL.
9. YOU SHALL NOT BEAR FALSE WITNESS.
10. YOU SHALL NOT COVET.

The Ten Commandments became the core of what was later developed and amplified into the Five Books of Moses (the *Pentateuch*). These Five Books, the first part of the Hebrew Scriptures (known as *Torah*), are often referred to as the Law. Later, many volumes were written in inter-pretations or commentaries on the Law.

The foundation of Judaism is a belief, an article of faith, upon which its doctrines and all Judaic ethics are based. The many variations of the central premise, the Articles of Faith set up much later, the basic Commandments of this religious experience, the prayers and rituals it established during almost four millennia of history—all begin with the unquestioned belief in One God:

"Hear, O Israel, the Lord our God, the Lord is One!"

This is known as the *Shemah* (the Name), with which Judaism begins and upon which it is founded.

3. Traces of the Past

In the Bible, particularly in the pre-Mosaic part, allusions are found to beliefs and practices that go back to early Semitic and prehistoric times—beliefs in animism, ancestor-worship, taboos, magic, polytheism, and an anthropomorphic concept of the gods.

In the animistic stage of religion it was believed that spirits took up their abode in trees, which became sacred and were worshiped. In the Bible we find Abraham, in his migration to Canaan, going to the "terebinth [a species of tree] of the Teacher." Later he builds an altar unto the Lord "by the terebinths of Mamre." Still later on, Abraham plants a tamarisk there and calls upon the name of the Lord. These references to the terebinth and the tamarisk reveal traces of an inheritance from the animistic worship of certain trees considered the dwelling places of spirits or deities.

God's first confrontation with Moses in the desert of Midian took place at the burning bush. When Moses wanted to examine the bush to learn why it burned and yet was not consumed, God called out from the midst of the bush and warned him: "Draw not nigh hither; put off thy shoes from off thy feet, for the place whereon thou standest is holy ground."

The distinguished scholar, W. A. E. Oesterly, in his book, *Hebrew Religion,* comments: "The account of the divine appearance at the burning bush is probably derived from two sources, Fire denoting the divine presence; and the bush as his abode." And he concludes: "A more pointed illustration of an echo of animistic belief could not be given."

Other passages in the early part of the Bible might be cited to show traces of the worship of running water as a medium of oracles; and stones considered to be the dwelling place of the divine spirit; and many instances of the use of magic.

Here is one example:

When Moses was sent down to Egypt to bring his people out of slavery, he asked for a sign that would convince them that God had sent him. This passage follows:

And the Lord said unto him: "What is that in thine hand?"

And he said: "A rod."

And the Lord said: "Cast it on the ground."

And he cast it on the ground and it became a serpent. And Moses fled from before it.

And the Lord said unto Moses: "Put forth thine hand, and take it by the tail."

And Moses put forth his hand, and caught it, and it became a rod in his hand.

4. The Thirteen Articles of Faith

Most of the beliefs and practices inherited from primitive Semitic religions have long been discarded by Judaism. But the belief in One God, introduced by Abraham, reinterpreted and redefined many times since, has remained constant. The nature of God and man's relationship to him have been frequently re-examined, re-explained and re-interpreted from Biblical times to the present day. But the existence of God, the belief in One God, was never subject to doubt or question. The *Shemah* was, and remains, the cornerstone of Judaism.

A Jewish philosopher, Philo of Alexandria, who lived in the first century A.D. (20 B.C.–A.D. 50), compressed the basic beliefs of Judaism into five fundamental concepts:

1. The belief in God;
2. The belief that there is only One God;
3. The belief that God created the world; but the world is not eternal;
4. The belief that there is only One universe; and
5. The belief that God cares for the world and all its creatures.

At an early period Judaism conceived of God in anthropomorphic terms. He was described in idealized, human terms. Since the Bible states that "God created man in his own image," from this it was concluded that God had physical attributes similar to those he had given to man: feet on which to walk; eyes with which to see; ears with which to hear; and a face which Moses saw when he spoke to Him "face to face." To God were also attributed the feelings experienced by man: love and hate, mercy and compassion, jealousy and vindictiveness.

This concept of God gradually gave way to the concept of an incorporeal Creator. And he was referred to by many names, each representing a special attribute. Often he is merely called, the Name. And the first symbolical and mystical name, designating that all Being comes from Him, has become the Name that no tongue may utter. It is ineffable and unutterable.

In the thirteenth century A.D., a philosopher, physician, and renowned Hebrew scholar, known as Moses ben Maimon, or Maimonides, opens his book, *The Guide for the Perplexed,* with a commentary to clarify the statement in the Bible that man is made in God's image. Some believed, Maimonides argues, that by the word "image," "the shape and figure of a thing is to be understood, and this explanation led men to believe in the corporeality (of the Divine Being): for they thought the words 'Let us make man in our image' implied that God had the form of a human being, i.e., that he had figure and shape, and that, consequently, He is corporeal. They adhered faithfully to this view, and thought that if they were to relinquish it they would *eo ipso* reject the truth of the Bible: and further, if they did not conceive God as having a body possessed of face and limbs, similar to their own in appearance, they would have to deny even the existence of God."

He goes on to explain that the phrase "Let us make man in our image" signifies not a physical likeness but an intellectual likeness. We find many instances in the Bible, he argues, where expressions are used such as: "He is like a lion"; "I am like a pelican of the wilderness"; "Their poison is like the poison of the serpent." The resemblances do not refer to figure and shape but to certain abstract comparisons.

And Maimonides concludes: "As man's distinction consists in a property which no other creature on earth possesses, viz., intellectual perception, in the exercise of which he does not employ his senses, nor move his hand or his foot, this perception has been compared—though apparently, not in truth—to the Divine perception, which requires no corporeal organ. On this account, i.e., on account of the Divine intellect with which man has been endowed, he is said to have been made in the form and likeness of the Almighty, but far from it be the notion that the Supreme Being is corporeal, having a material form."

With this basic belief that God is not corporeal, but that he is omnipotent, omniscient, and eternal, Judaism begins the elaboration of its entire set of beliefs.

Maimonides reduced Judaism to Thirteen Articles of Faith. Though not officially adopted, this Credo was incorporated into the Daily Prayerbook. The Credo reads:

1. I believe with perfect faith that the Creator, blessed be His Name, is the Creator and Guide of everything that

has been created, and He alone has made, does make, and will make all things.

2. I believe with perfect faith that the Creator, blessed be His Name, is One, and that there is no unity in any manner like unto His, and that He alone is our God, who was, and is, and will be.

3. I believe with perfect faith that the Creator, blessed be His Name, is not a body, and that He is free from all the properties of matter, and that He has not any form whatever.

4. I believe with perfect faith that the Creator, blessed be His Name, is the first and the last.

5. I believe with perfect faith that to the Creator, blessed be His Name, and to Him alone, it is right to pray, and that it is not right to pray to any being besides Him.

6. I believe with perfect faith that all the words of the prophets are true.

7. I believe with perfect faith that the prophecy of Moses, our teacher, peace be unto him, was true, and that he was the chief of the prophets, both of those who preceded and of those who followed him.

8. I believe with perfect faith that the whole *Torah,* now in our possession, is the same that was given to Moses, our teacher, peace be unto him.

9. I believe with perfect faith that this Torah will not be changed, and that there will never be any other Law from the Creator, blessed be His Name.

10. I believe with perfect faith that the Creator, blessed be His Name, knows every deed of the children of men, and all their thoughts, as it is said. It is He that fashioned the hearts of them all, that gives heed to all their works.

11. I believe with perfect faith that the Creator, blessed be His Name, rewards those that keep His commandments and punishes those that transgress them.

12. I believe with perfect faith in the coming of the Messiah; and, though he tarry, I will wait daily for his coming.

13. I believe with perfect faith that there will be a revival of the dead at the time when it shall please the Creator, blessed be His Name, and exalted be His Fame for ever and ever.

For Thy salvation I hope, O Lord.

Some of these Articles of Faith were subjected to criticism. But the first three remained unquestioned:

The belief in God as Creator;

The belief in the Unity of God;

The belief in the incorporeality of God.

The existence of the Creator is proven by the order in the universe. And many of the qualities attributed to Him are enumerated in the prayers. Since man was created in His image by the endowment of intellectual perception, man is obliged to aspire to be as godly as possible within the scope of his dual nature.

5. Upon What Does the World Rest?

In Judaism some of the attributes of God, which are infinite in number, are represented in His names. He is called: the Holy One; Creator of the World; Master of the World; Lord of Hosts; the Rock; Gracious Lord; Source of All Truth; and so on. Above all, he is extolled as God of Justice. The belief in God's justice is repeated in the Bible and in post-Biblical literature many times. And the idea is amplified by the Prophets. In the *Talmud,* which is an elaboration and commentary on the Oral Law, this statement is found: "Upon what does the world rest? Upon a single pillar and its name is: Justice."

Since man is considered to resemble God only to the extent that he is given the faculty to aspire to be God-like, and since justice is a primary attribute of God, it follows that man must strive to deal justly.

The Just Man, in Judaism, is revered much as the Saint, the Guru, the Superior Man, the Man of Courage, is revered in other religions. And there is a belief that the world is preserved for the sake of the Just Man.

According to a Rabbinic legend, when the flood subsided in the days of Noah, God made a covenant with Noah and his children never again to destroy all living creatures. And he created seventy-two just men. Thirty-six were placed in heaven to plead for the erring brothers on earth; and thirty-six are scattered throughout the world, so that when the corruption of man grows great, the Lord remembers the thirty-six just men, and for their sake he spares mankind.

That justice is a cardinal virtue is repeated in the Bible many times. And the Prophet Micah sums up this basic belief: "What does the Lord require of you? Only to do justly: to love mercy; and to walk humbly with your God."

6. Heaven Is Not "Up"

Charity, and how it should be practiced, is returned to often in the Bible and is given importance in the commentaries. This virtue is considered so great that no man is to be regarded as so poor as not to be obligated to practice it. It is the moral duty of each individual. This includes helping the widowed and the orphaned; providing education for those unable to obtain it; caring for the sick; easing the burden of the needy. Early in the Bible there is the injunction: "Open wide your hand to your brother, to the needy and to the poor." And on all joyful and mournful occasions it is traditionally incumbent upon both celebrants and mourners to distribute charity.

There is a Judaic legend which illustrates the importance given to the practice of charity in the religion of Judaism:

When the Jews returned from captivity to rebuild their land, their Holy City and their Temple, there lived a Jew in Egypt named Nittai, who was a gatherer of books.

He prepared to go for a trip one day and sent his servant to buy a camel and a saddle. The servant returned and when the saddle was removed from the camel, a fortune in rare diamonds was discovered hidden in a pouch. Nittai sent the diamonds back to the camel dealer with the message:

"I bought a camel and a saddle, but not these jewels."

The grateful merchant came to thank Nittai. "Had you kept them," he said, "I could not have brought you to court."

"That is true. But had I kept them, I would have lost my integrity. One can enter the Heavenly Kingdom without diamonds, but not without honesty."

"I have heard about this 'Heavenly Kingdom,'" said the camel dealer. "How does one get up there?"

"First, my son, heaven is neither 'up' or 'down,' but in our hearts," said Nittai. "The way to reach it is through good deeds; and the best road of all is through charity. These are the eight stations along the road to the Heavenly Kingdom:

"The first is reached by him who gives charity with his hand but not with his heart;

"The second station is reached by him who gives with his hand and his heart but not generously;

"The third station is reached by him who gives generously with hand and heart, but not until he is asked;

"The fourth station is reached by him who gives generously

without being asked, but gives directly to those in need and thereby causes them humiliation and shame;

"The fifth station is reached by him who gives generously, without being asked, and in a manner that the giver does not know the receiver, but the receiver knows the giver;

"The sixth station is reached by him who gives generously, and knows the receiver, but the receiver does not know the giver;

"The seventh station is reached by him who gives generously, and both receiver and giver do not know each other;

"And the eighth station is reached by him who gives charity to keep people from ever needing charity.

"And that is the road to the Heavenly Kingdom."

"What you have taught me," said the camel dealer, "is of greater worth than those jewels. And I want to give them to you to show my gratitude."

"I have already been rewarded in seeing the seed of my words take root so quickly. Therefore, if you wish to give the jewels away, give them to Governor Nehemiah in Jerusalem and he will use them in a worthy cause."

7. Where Does the Soul Go?

When a man dies, according to Judaism, the mortal body is buried in the ground, for man, created from dust, is returned to dust. And the soul of the good man ascends to his Maker. If the man was evil, the soul descends to hell (*Gehinnon*), where punishment is meted out for sins committed. When cleansed of all sins, the purified soul ascends to heaven.

No mention is made of a life hereafter in the early period of Judaism as given in the Hebrew Scriptures. But the Jews exiled to Babylon, who came in contact with other cultures, adopted, and adapted, this belief. In *The Sayings of the Fathers*, written between 300 B.C. and A.D. 200, the statement appears that: "This world is like a vestibule before the World to Come." And since then a vast Rabbinic literature has arisen of speculations on all aspects of life after death.

During their many years of troubled history, the Jewish people began to anticipate the coming of a Redeemer, a Messiah, who would establish heaven on earth, and forever secure Zion as the holy city. On that day, all the dead would be revived.

By the time Maimonides drew up his Articles of Faith, he incorporated these beliefs: one in the resurrection of the dead; and the other in the coming of the Messiah.

8. Who Knows One?

Interwoven into the fabric of Judaism are constant reminders of God and man's dependence upon him. Three times daily in his prayers the observant Jew repeats the *Shemah*. And fastened to the doorpost of his house there is a small case made of wood or metal, called a *mezuzah,* which contains two quotations from Deuteronomy, taken from the second discourse of Moses. The first one reads:

Hear, O Israel, the Lord our God is One. And you shall love the Lord your God with all your heart and with all your soul and with all your might. And these words which I command you this day shall be in your heart.

In the second and lengthier quotation, Moses beseeches them to follow the Commandments, to love the Lord, and to teach his words to their children. Toward the end he exhorts them to write his words "upon the doorposts of thine house, and upon thy gates."

Each time, upon coming in or going out, the *mezuzah* is touched with the tips of two fingers, which are then kissed —in this way prompted to be mindful of God in all goings-out and comings-in.

In the twentieth century, and particularly since World War II, it has become customary among Jewish soldiers to wear a *mezuzah* around their neck as an ornament, or as a religious identification.

There is one ritual in which the entire family takes part, which is held on the first night of the annual Feast of Passover, celebrating the emancipation of the Jews from Egyptian slavery some 3500 years ago. The celebration is meant primarily for the young, so that the story of the *Exodus* may be kept alive and handed down from generation to generation. Since the festivity is intended for the young, the symbols are embodied in the food which is traditionally served, in the answers to questions which are ritually asked by the young, and in simple songs that delight the children and which impress upon them the basic beliefs of Judaism.

The Passover Eve ritual is written down for all to follow in a little book called *The Story of Passover (Haggadah Shel Pesach).* This gives the service in fifteen stages, as formal as a Japanese religious *Noh* play. It begins with a benediction over a cup of wine, and part of the first chapter of Genesis is sung according to a traditional mode. And it ends, hours later, with a concluding prayer which asks for God's approval of the service.

Early in the ceremony the youngest son (or youngest member of the family) addresses his father (or grandfather) and asks four questions. The first question is:

"How does this night differ from all other nights (in the year)?"

And his elder answers: "We were slaves to Pharaoh in Egypt (long, long ago), and the Lord our God brought us out of there with a strong hand and an outstretched arm. . . ."

The narrative continues, followed by a number of traditional and symbolical acts and songs, all directed to the young. Toward the end of the service, the elder and leader of the festive ritual asks in song form a set of riddles. All the celebrants join in singing the answers, and the last line is given in a crescendo. The answers underscore some of the basic beliefs of Judaism.

This song, freely translated, goes:

"Who knows one?" (What does "one" stand for?)
"I know one, One is our Lord, ruler of heaven and earth!"
"Who knows two?"
"I know two. Two are the Tablets of the Covenant. One is our Lord, ruler of heaven and earth!"
"Who knows three?"
"I know three. Three are the fathers.[1] Two are the Tablets of the Covenant. One is our Lord, ruler of heaven and earth!"

The song goes on and ends with:

"Who knows twelve?"
"I know twelve. Twelve are the Twelve Tribes. Eleven are the stars in Joseph's dream. Ten are the Ten Commandments. Nine are the months of gestation. Eight are the days of circumcision. Seven are the days of the Sabbath-week. Six are the books of the Mishnah.[2] Five are the Books of the *Torah*.[3] Four are the Mothers.[4] Three are the fathers. Two are the Tablets of the Covenant. One is our Lord, ruler of heaven and earth!"

Here is one instance of many in which the young are taught the beliefs of Judaism, and in which emphasis is given to the basic belief—the belief in One God.

[1]) Fathers: Abraham, Isaac and Jacob. [2]) Mishnah: Oral Law.
[3]) Torah: The Five Books of Moses. [4]) Mothers: Sarah, Rebekah, Rachel and Leah.

9. What Judaism Believes

The beliefs of Judaism have gone through a number of changes from the beginning to the present. Some beliefs and rituals have been abandoned. Some have been transformed and assumed new meaning through contact with the different civilizations and cultures in which Jews found refuge and thrived. Some antiquated beliefs, formalized in tradition, linger on as a heritage of the past and still find devoted followers who cling to them.

Certain basic beliefs which characterize Judaism have survived the many changes in ritual and tradition, and the differences between Orthodox, Conservative and Reform Judaism. These basic beliefs on which Judaism as a faith continues are:

The belief in One God—Who is eternal, Creator and Preserver of all that is in the universe;

That God is incorporeal;

That God, the Creator, is Judge and Arbiter of everyone's ultimate destiny;

That man was created with a mortal body and an immortal soul;

That man has a dual nature and is ruled by two impulses: one good, and the other evil;

That man is born with a free will, and has the choice between good and evil;

That man is born innocent—and as long as he conquers his evil impulses, he remains innocent;

That all life is to be revered, because all life is God-given;

That justice is a cardinal virtue—for God is just;

That truth is a cardinal virtue—for without truth justice cannot be done;

That Peace is indispensable—for the world rests on Justice, Truth and Peace;

That the Ten Commandments were revealed to Moses as a guide and law for all mankind.

10. The Code of Holiness

There is a code in Leviticus which gives the basic teachings on fulfilling the Divine will. This is known as *The Code of Holiness:*

You shall be holy, for I the Lord your God am holy!

Every one among you shall revere his father and his mother. You shall rise up before the hoary head, and honor the face of the old man.

You shall not steal, nor deal falsely, nor lie one to another. And you shall not swear by my name falsely: I am the Lord.

You shall not oppress your neighbor, nor defraud him. The wages of him who is hired shall not abide with you all night until the morrow.

You shall do no injustice in weight or in measure. Just weights and balances shall you have.

And when you reap the harvest of your land, you shall not wholly reap the corners of your field, nor gather the gleanings after your harvest. And you shall not glean your vineyard, nor gather its fallen fruit; you shall leave them for the poor and the stranger.

You shall not curse the deaf, nor put a stumbling block before the blind.

You shall do no injustice in judgment; you shall not be partial toward the person of the poor, nor favor the person of the mighty, but in righteousness shall you judge your neighbor.

You shall not be a talebearer; neither shall you stand idly by the blood of your neighbor.

You shall not hate your brother in your heart, nor shall you rebuke him so as to cause sin upon him.

You shall seek no vengeance, nor bear a grudge, but you shall love your neighbor as yourself: I am the Lord.

You shall keep my Sabbaths, and reverence my sanctuary.

And when a stranger dwells in your land, you shall not wrong him. The stranger among you shall be to you as the home born among you, and you shall love him as yourself.

11. From the Book of Job

There is a dramatic poem in the Hebrew Scriptures which centers about an afflicted man named Job, who questions the justice of God.

The Book of Job was so highly regarded by the Ancients, that its authorship was ascribed to Moses.

This brief extract indicates the involvement with the concept of justice, and the rich imagery used to suggest the majesty of the Creator:

Job speaks:

"I cry to you, and you do not answer; I stand up, and

you do not look at me! You have become cruel to me; with the might of your hand you persecute me. You lift me up to the wind; you make me ride upon it, and dissolve my substance in the storm. Why? Did I not weep for him who was in trouble? Was not my soul grieved for the poor? Yet when I looked for good, evil came to me; and when I waited for light there came darkness. My harp has turned to mourning, my lute to the voice of those who weep."

Then the Lord answered Job out of the whirlwind:

"Who is this that darkens counsel by words without knowledge? Gird up your loins like a man; for I will ask of you, and you shall answer me:

"Where were you when I laid the foundation of the earth? Declare, if you have the understanding. Who determined its measures, if you know? Upon what were the foundations fastened, and who laid its cornerstone, when the morning stars sang together, and all the sons of God shouted for joy? Who restricted the sea with boundaries when it broke forth as if it had issued from the womb, when I made the cloud its garment, and a swaddling band for it of thick darkness, and prescribed for it my decree, and set bars and doors, and said, This far shall you come, but no further, and here shall your proud waves be stayed?

"Have you ever commanded the morning, and caused the daybreak to know its place, that it might take hold of the ends of the earth and shake the wicked out of it? Have you entered into the springs of the sea? Or searched the recesses of the deep? Have the gates of death been revealed to you, or the doors of the shadow of death? Can you show me the way to the dwelling of light, and to the house of darkness, that you may follow it to its boundaries? Have you entered the treasuries of the snow, or seen the storehouse of the hail which I have reserved against time of trouble, against the day of battle?

"Show me the place where the light parts, or the east wind scatters upon the earth. Who has divided the torrents, and made a way for the lightning of the thunder, to cause it to rain upon the earth, and satisfy the waste and desolate ground, and make the tender grass to grow? Who has begotten drops of dew, or drops of rain? Out of whose womb came the ice? Who has gendered the hoary frost of heaven, and covered the waters as with stone, and caused the face of the deep to be frozen?

"Can you bind the cluster of the Pleiades, or loose the bands of Orion? Know you the laws of the heavens? Can you lift up your voice to the clouds and command them, that abundance of waters may cover you? Who has put wisdom in the mind, or understanding in the heart? Will you hunt the prey for the lioness, or satisfy the appetite of the young lions when they crouch in their dens? Who provides food for the raven when his young ones cry to God and wander for lack of food?

"Know you the time when the wild goats of the rock bring forth? Or when the hinds calve? Who has set the wild ass free, and made the wilderness his home, and the salt land his dwelling place, and the mountains his pasture? Will the unicorn be content to serve you, and abide by your crib? Can you bind him with his band in the furrow, and will he harrow the valleys for you? Will you trust him because his strength is great, to bring home your seed, and gather the grain of the threshing floor? Gave you wings to the peacock, or feathers to the ostrich?

"Have you given the horse his height? Have you clothed his neck with quivering power? Can you make him leap as a young grasshopper? The glory of his snorting is terrible. He paws in the valley and rejoices in his strength; he goes out to meet the armed men. He mocks at fear and turns not back from the sword. The quiver rattles against him, the glittering shield and the spear; yet he swallows the ground with fierceness and rage at the sound of the trumpet and the smell of battle.

"Does the hawk soar by your wisdom, and stretch her wings toward the south? Does the eagle mount at your command, and make her nest high upon the crag of the rock? From there she spies her prey, and where the slain are, there is she.

"Behold now the behemoth, which I made with man! He eats grass like an ox; but observe the strength in his loins, and the force in the muscles of his belly. His tail is like a cedar, and the sinews of his thighs are closely knit together. His bones are like rods of brass or bars of iron. Only he who made him can make the sword to approach him. Surely the mountains bring forth food for him, where all the beasts of the field do play. He lies down in the shadow among the reeds and tall grass; the willows of the brook surround him. He drains a lake to slake his thirst, he hastens not; he is confident he can drink the Jordan dry. Can you take him by his eyes, or pierce his nose with a nose-ring?

"Can you draw out the leviathan with a fishhook? Shall your friends make a banquet of him, or divide him among the merchants? Can you fill his skin with barbed irons or his head with fish spears? If you try to lay your hand upon him, and remember the battle, you will not try it again! Shall not one be cast down even at the sight of him?

"None is so fierce who dares stir him up; who then is able to stand before me? Whatsoever is under the whole heaven is mine!"

Then Job answered the Lord and said:

"I know that you can do all things, and that no thought can be hidden from you. I have uttered that which I understood not, things too wonderful for me, which I knew not. Hear, I beseech you, and I will speak. I have heard of you by the hearing of the ear, but now my eye sees you. Therefore I abhor myself, and repent in dust and ashes!"

12. From the Book of Prophets

Judaism is a religion of many prophets. There are the prophets who spoke *with* God, called "The Former Prophets" (from Adam and Abraham to Elisha and Elijah); and those who spoke *for* God, known as "The Latter Prophets" (from Isaiah and Jeremiah to Joel and Jonah).

The Latter Prophets, as given in the Bible, were inspired poets who would appear before the people to admonish them when they departed from the Commandments, or to comfort them in their time of trouble.

The laws of justice and truth were kept burnished bright for the people by the poetry of the prophets:

● SWORDS INTO PLOWSHARES

It shall come to pass, in the latter days, that the house of the Lord shall be established at the top of the mountains; and all nations shall flow to it; and many people shall come and say:

"Let us go up to the mountain of the Lord, to the house of the God of Jacob! And he will teach us his ways, that we may walk in his paths. For out of Zion shall go forth the law, and the word of the Lord from Jerusalem."

Then shall he judge the nations and rebuke many peoples; and they shall beat their swords into plowshares, and their spears into pruning hooks; nation shall not lift up sword against nation; neither shall they learn war any more.

Isaiah

● THE LORD ALONE SHALL BE EXALTED

Enter into the rock, and hide yourself in the dust, for fear of the Lord and for the glory of his majesty. For the day of the Lord of hosts shall come upon the proud and lofty as well as on those who have been brought low; upon all the cedars of Lebanon, so high, and upon the oaks of Bashan; upon the high mountains and every high tower; upon every fortified wall, and all the ships of Tarshish.

The proud shall be bowed down and the haughty made low, and the Lord alone shall be exalted in that day.

In that day a man shall take his idols of silver and his idols of gold, which he made for himself to worship, and cast them to the moles and the bats, and hide them in the clefts of the rocks, for fear of the Lord and for the glory of his majesty, when he arises to shake the earth terribly.

Isaiah

● THE EYES OF THE BLIND

Say to those fearful of heart, "Be strong, fear not! Behold, your God will come and save you!"

Then the eyes of the blind shall be opened, and the ears of the deaf unstopped. The lame man shall leap like a hart, and the tongue of the dumb sing out. The waters shall break out in the wilderness, and streams in the desert; the parched ground shall become like a pool, and the thirsty land like springs of water. In the haunt of jackals, herds shall gather; there the grass and reeds and rushes shall grow.

And a highway shall be there, and it shall be called the holy way. The unclean shall not pass over it; but it shall be for God's wayfarers. And even fools shall not err upon it. No lion shall be found there, nor any ravenous beast; but the redeemed shall walk there, the ransomed of the Lord shall return by it. And they shall come to Zion with songs upon their lips, and everlasting joy upon their heads. They shall find joy and gladness, and sorrow and sighing shall flee away.

Isaiah

● WHO HAS MEASURED THE WATERS

Who has measured the waters in the hollow of his hand, and computed the heavens with a span, and meted out the dust of the earth in a measure, and weighed the mountains in scales, and the hills in a balance?

Who has probed the spirit of the Lord, or, as his counselor, has taught him? Whose counsel has he sought; and who instructed him in judgment and taught him in knowledge, and pointed out the way of understanding?

Lo, to him all the nations are as a drop from a bucket, or accounted as fine dust on a scale; the weight of the islands are a mote to him, and the whole of Lebanon not enough for fuel, nor its beasts for a burnt offering. All the nations are as nothing before him; as less than nothing are they accounted.

To whom, then, will you liken God? The idol cast by the smelter, and overlaid with gold by the goldsmith? Do you not know, or have you not heard, and were you not told from the beginning—since the foundation of the earth was established—that it is the Lord who sits above the circle of the earth, and all its inhabitants are as grasshoppers? It is he who stretched out the heavens like a curtain, and spread them like a tent to dwell in; it is he who brings princes to nothing, and turns to naught judges of the earth. Scarcely are they planted, scarcely are they sown, and scarcely has their stock taken root in the earth, when he blows upon them and they wither, and the whirlwind carries them away like straw.

Why do you say, O Jacob, and you, O Israel, "My way is hidden from the Lord; justice is passed over by my God"? Do you not know, and have you not heard, that the everlasting God, the Creator of the earth, neither weakens nor wearies, that his understanding is beyond probing? It is he who gives strength to the weak; and to the weary, power. Even youths grow faint and weary, and young men fall; but those who wait upon the Lord renew their strength, they mount up as on the wings of eagles; and those who trust in the Lord shall run and not tire, they shall go on and not grow faint.

Isaiah

• THE MAN WHO FEEDS ON ASHES

A man hews down a cedar, or an oak or a cypress, which the Lord planted and the rain nourished; and he takes part of the tree for fuel, and kindles a fire and bakes bread; and of the rest he carves an idol, and bows down before it and worships it, and prays to it, saying, "Deliver me, for you are my god!"

But he does not consider in his heart to say, "Is there knowledge or understanding in him who says, 'Half of the tree I burned in the fire, and on its embers I baked bread and roasted meat; and the rest I shall make into an idol and bow down before the block of wood.' "

That man feeds on ashes, and has been misled, so that he can no longer save himself and say, "Is there not a lie in my right hand?"

Isaiah

● THE CALL OF THE PROPHET

The spirit of the Lord God is upon me, because the Lord has anointed me to bring good tidings to the humble. He has sent me to bind up the brokenhearted, to proclaim liberty to the captives, to open the gates for those who are imprisoned, to comfort all who mourn, and to give to the mourners in Zion beauty instead of ashes, the oil of joy instead of sorrow, the mantle of praise in place of the garment of dejection; that they may be called "the trees of righteousness," "the planting of the Lord," in which he may be glorified.

As a bridegroom puts on his diadem, and a bride adorns herself with her jewels, as the earth in spring brings forth her shoots, so the Lord God will cause justice and praise to spring forth among the nations.

Isaiah

● BLESSED IS THE MAN

Cursed is the man who trusts in man, who makes flesh his strength and whose heart turns away from the Lord. He shall be like a tree in the desert, in the parched places of the wilderness, in a salt land, uninhabited.

Blessed is the man who trusts in the Lord and whose hope is the Lord. He shall be like a tree planted by the river, which spreads its roots in the waters and fears not when heat comes, but whose leaves are ever green; not anxious in the year of drought, and never ceasing to yield fruit.

Jeremiah

● HAVE WE NOT ALL ONE FATHER?

Have we not all one Father? Has not one God created us all? Why then do we deal treacherously, every man against his brother, and profane the covenant of our fathers?

You have wearied the Lord with your words. Yet you say, "How have we wearied him?" When you say, "Everyone who does evil is good in the sight of the Lord, and he delights in them"; or when you ask, "Where is the God of justice?"

Malachi

13. From the Book of Psalms

This slender book has been called "A Bible in Miniature." It consists of one hundred and fifty Psalms that differ greatly in length. Some are very short like Psalm 117, which in the original Hebrew consists of four short lines. Others are very long like Psalm 119, which has one hundred and seventy-six couplets. Some are songs in praise of wisdom; some are in praise of victory; but most extol the majesty and glory of God.

That God is near and that man can commune with Him through prayer has been stressed from the earliest period of Judaism. At first prayer accompanied sacrifices. But later prayer replaced sacrifices. There are prayers of thanks and of supplication, confessions of collective sins and transgressions, silent prayers, and prayers to be sung or chanted by the congregation. But prayers in the glorification of the name are the dominant prayers.

● THE LORD IS MY SHEPHERD

The Lord is my shepherd; I shall not want.

He makes me to lie down in green pastures; he leads me beside the still waters; he restores my soul.

He leads me in the paths of righteousness for his name's sake.

Even though I walk through the valley of the shadow of death, I will fear no evil, for you are with me; your rod and your staff, they comfort me.

You prepare a table before me in the presence of my enemies; you anoint my head with oil; and my cup runs over.

Surely goodness and mercy shall follow me all the days of my life, and I will dwell in the house of the Lord forever.

Psalm 23

● LET THE NATIONS BE GLAD

God be merciful to us, and bless us, and cause his face to shine upon us; that your way may be known upon earth, your saving health among all nations!

Let the peoples praise you, O God; let all the peoples praise you. O let the nations be glad and sing for joy, for you shall judge the people justly and govern the nations upon earth.

Let the peoples praise you, O God; let all the peoples praise you. The earth has yielded her increase; may God, our God, bless us!

Psalm 67

● O COME, LET US WORSHIP

O come, let us sing to the Lord; let us shout for joy to the Rock of our salvation! Let us come before his presence with thanksgiving, and shout joyfully to him with psalms.

For the Lord is a great God. In his hand are the depths of the earth; the heights of the hills are his also. The sea is his and he made it, and his hands formed the dry land.

O come, let us worship and bow down; let us kneel before the Lord our Maker! For he is our God, and we are the people of his pasture and the sheep of his hand.

Psalm 95

● WHEN THE LORD BROUGHT BACK THE CAPTIVES

When the Lord brought back the captives to Zion, we were like those who dream. Then was our mouth filled with laughter, and our tongue with singing. Then said they among the nations, "The Lord has done great things for them!"

The Lord has done great things for us, and we are glad.

Turn again our captivity, O Lord, as the streams in the dry land.

Those who sow in tears shall reap in joy; and he who goes forth and weeps, bearing precious seed, shall return with rejoicing, bearing his sheaves with him.

Psalm 126

● LIKE THE DEW OF HERMON

Behold, how good and how pleasant it is for brothers to dwell together in unity!

It is like precious ointment; it is like the dew of Hermon that descends upon the mountains of Zion. For there the Lord commanded the blessing: life forevermore.

Psalm 133

● IF I TAKE WING WITH THE MORNING STAR

O Lord, you have searched me and known me. You know when I sit down and when I rise up; you understand my thoughts from afar. There is not a word in my tongue, but lo, O Lord, you know it. Such knowledge is too wonderful for me; it is too high. I cannot attain to it.

Where shall I go, and whither shall I flee from your presence? If I ascend into heaven, you are there, and if I make my bed in Sheol, behold, you are there. If I take wing with the morning star, and dwell in the uttermost parts of the sea, even there would your hand lead me, and your right hand hold me. If I say, "Surely the darkness will cover me," even night becomes light about me; yes, the darkness hides nothing from you. The darkness and the light are both alike to you.

Marvelous are your works; and that my soul knows well. And in your book all the days of my life are recorded. How precious are your thoughts to me, O God! How great is the sum of them! Were I to count them, they would outnumber the sands.

Search me, O God, and know my heart! Try me, and know my thoughts! See if there is any wicked way in me, and lead me to your way everlasting.

Psalm 139

● PRAISE THE LORD

> Praise the Lord!
> Praise God in his sanctuary;
> Praise him in the firmament of his power;
> Praise him for his mighty acts;
> Praise him according to his greatness!
> Praise him with the sound of the trumpet;
> Praise him with psaltery and harp.
> Praise him with the timbrel and dance;
> Praise him with stringed instruments and pipes;
> Praise him upon the crashing cymbals.
> Let everything that has breath praise the Lord!
> Hallelujah!
> *Psalm 150*

14. Sayings from the Hebrew Scriptures

Shall not the Judge of all the world do justly?
You shall not follow a multitude to do evil.
Have one law for the sojourner and for the native.
If your brother becomes poor and cannot maintain himself, you shall maintain him.

The bows of the mighty are broken, but the feeble gird on strength.

Wickedness proceeds from the wicked.

Eat the fat, and drink the sweet, and send portions to those for whom nothing is prepared.

The Lord gave and the Lord has taken away; blessed be the name of the Lord.

The triumph of the wicked is short, and the joy of the godless but for a moment.

The price of wisdom is above pearls.

To depart from evil is understanding.

The earth is the Lord's, and the fullness thereof.

Weeping may endure for a night, but joy comes in the morning.

The humble shall inherit the earth.

Cast your burden upon the Lord, and he will sustain you.

Except the Lord build the house, they labor in vain who build it.

Say not to your neighbor, "Go, and come again, and tomorrow I will give," when you have it with you.

Envy not the man of violence, and choose none of his ways.

His own iniquities will ensnare the wicked, and he will be held with the cords of his sin.

Go to the ant, you sluggard; consider her ways, and be wise; who having no chief, overseer, or ruler, provides her bread in the summer, and gathers her food in the harvest.

There are six things which the Lord hates, seven which are an abomination to him: haughty eyes, a lying tongue, and hands that shed innocent blood; a heart that devises wicked thoughts, feet that are swift in running to evil; a false witness that breathes out lies, and he who sows discord among brothers.

Can a man take fire in his bosom, and his clothes not be burned? Or can one walk upon hot coals, and his feet not be scorched? So he who seeks his neighbor's wife; whoever touches her shall not go unpunished.

A friend loves at all times, and a brother is born for adversity.

The woman Folly is clamorous; she is thoughtless, and knows nothing. And to him who lacks understanding, she says, "Stolen waters are sweet, and bread eaten in secret is pleasant." But he knows not that the dead are there; that her guests are in the depths of hell.

Hatred stirs up strife, but love covers all sins.

For want of guidance a people will fall, but in many counselors there is safety.

The generous soul shall be enriched; and he who satisfies shall himself be satisfied.

A good woman is a crown to her husband.

A righteous man has regard for the life of his beast, but even the tender mercies of the wicked are cruel.

Hope deferred makes the heart sick, but desire fulfilled is a tree of life.

A tranquil heart prolongs life, but envy is a rot in the bones.

He who oppresses the poor blasphemes his Maker, but he who has mercy on the needy honors Him.

A soft answer turns away wrath, but harsh words stir up anger.

All the days of the poor are sorrowful, but he of a merry heart has a continual feast.

Better a dinner of herbs where love is, than a roasted ox, with hatred.

To the wise the path of life goes upward.

He who is slow to anger is better than the mighty, and he who rules his temper than he who conquers a city.

The lot is cast, but disposing of it is from the Lord.

He who rewards evil for good, evil shall not depart from his house.

He who finds a good wife finds a great good, and obtains favor of the Lord.

There are many devices in a man's heart, but it is the purpose of the Lord that shall be established.

Who can say, "I have made my heart clean, I am pure from my sin?"

The lazy man says, "There's a lion in the street; I will be killed if I go out."

Remove not the ancient landmark which your fathers have set.

As he thinks in his heart, so is he.

Who has woe? Who has sorrow? Who has strife? Who has wounds without cause? Who has redness of the eyes? Those who tarry long over wine. Look not upon the wine when it is red, when it gives its color to the cup. It may slide down smoothly, but in the end it bites like a serpent, and stings like an adder.

Through wisdom a house is built, and by understanding it is established, and by knowledge the chambers are filled with all precious and pleasant riches.

Rejoice not when your enemy falls, and let not your heart be glad when he stumbles.

I went by the field of the slothful, and by the vineyard of the man void of understanding. And lo, it was overgrown with thistles, and covered with nettles, and the stone wall was broken down. Then I beheld, and considered; I saw, and received instruction. "Yet a little sleep, a little slumber, a little folding of the hands to sleep"—so shall poverty come upon you like a runner, and want, like an armed man.

If your enemy is hungry, give him bread to eat, and if he is thirsty, give him water to drink: for you will heap coals of fire upon his head, and the Lord will reward you.

He who cannot control his temper is like a city without defenses.

The eyes of man are never satisfied.

The wicked flee when no man pursues, but the righteous are bold as a lion.

Where there is no vision, the people perish.

A man's pride shall bring him low, but the humble in spirit shall obtain honor.

Give strong drink to him who is ready to perish, and wine to those heavy of heart.

All the rivers run into the sea, yet the sea is not full; to the place from where the rivers come, there they return again.

To everything there is a season, and a time to every purpose under the heaven: a time to be born, and a time to die; a time to plant, and a time to pluck up that which is planted.

God made man upright, but they have sought out many inventions.

Cast your bread upon the waters: for you shall find it after many days.

He who observes the wind shall not sow, and he who regards the clouds shall not reap.

Remember then your Creator in the days of your youth; before the silver cord is loosed, or the golden bowl is broken, or the pitcher is broken at the fountain, or the wheel broken at the cistern; and the dust returns to the earth as it was, and the spirit returns to God who gave it.

The grass dies up, the flower fades, only the word of the Lord endures forever.

How beautiful upon the mountains are the feet of him who brings good tidings, who publishes peace!

Let justice flow like waters, and righteousness like a mighty stream.

As you have done, it shall be done to you.

O man, what is good, and what does the Lord require of you? Only to do justly; to love mercy; and to walk humbly with your God.

Have we not all one Father? Has not one God created us all?

9 CHRISTIANITY

Religion of One Third of Humanity

1. The Story of Jesus

Christianity is the faith that has the largest following in the world. And it begins with the story of its founder, Jesus of Nazareth.

Today the story of Jesus is better known to a greater number of people throughout the world than any other in human history. The very name (though there were many so named in his period and have been many more since) evokes associations and emotion; and to many the mere repetition of the name is a harbinger of good fortune and a blessing—as is the repetition of the name "Rama" to the followers of Hinduism. Jesus is known to Christians by a great number of beatific names, and is adored by his followers with an intimacy akin to that of children for their father.

It is generally accepted that Jesus was born about 7–5 B.C. in Judea, a small country in Asia Minor, at a time when it had come under the rule of Rome and was in a state of great unrest. The people, rich and poor, young and old, learned and ignorant, speculated hopefully about the coming of the Messiah, who would redeem the Jews from their oppressors and bring peace to the world. They did not know where and how the Messiah would appear, but they were convinced that the troubled times in which they lived were omens and signs which indicated the immanence of his coming.

And at this time of tense expectancy Jesus was born. He grew up in Nazareth, a town in lower Galilee, some fifty-five miles from Jerusalem. And there he was taught the Holy Law of Judaism and the traditions of his people.

Yet though these basic facts of his life, with some variations, are accepted—of the historical Jesus we have scant information, other than that given in the four Gospels at the beginning of the New Testament. The Gospel according to *John,* "the Beloved Disciple," concerns primarily the spiritual life and teachings of Jesus rather than the story of his life. The other three Gospels, according to *Matthew*, *Mark* and *Luke*, if placed in parallel columns, present the same story (in different literary styles), often duplicating and sometimes supplementing each other. They are known as the Synoptic Gospels.

From the Synoptic Gospels we learn dimly where and when and under what conditions Jesus was born. In *Mark*, the oldest of the Gospels, nothing is recorded of the birth or youth of Jesus, for it begins when he came to the river Jordan and appeared before John the Baptist at the age of about thirty. *Matthew* adds little to illuminate the early life of Jesus. Only *Luke* who, as he tells us at the outset, had known of many earlier narratives, gives fuller and greater detail, presumably gleaned from the earlier Gospels "just as they were delivered to us by those who from the beginning were eyewitnesses and ministers of the word."

In his own narrative *Luke* relates that Jesus, at the age of twelve, went with his parents from the town of Nazareth to the city of Jerusalem for the celebration of the feast of the Passover, which brought pilgrims from all over the country.

And when the feast was ended, as they were returning, the boy Jesus stayed behind in Jerusalem. His parents did not know it, but supposing him to be in the company they went a day's journey, and they sought him among their kinsfolk and acquaintances; and when they did not find him, they returned to Jerusalem, seeking him. After three days they found him in the temple, sitting among the teachers, listening to them and asking them questions; and all who heard him were amazed at his understanding and his answers. And when they saw him they were astonished; and his mother said to him, "Son, why have you treated us so? Behold, your father and I have been looking for you anxiously." And he said to them, "How is it that you sought me? Did you not know that I must be in my Father's house?" And they did not understand the saying which he spoke to them.

Luke adds that after their return to Nazareth, "Jesus increased in wisdom and in stature, and in favor with God and man."

In the next chapter *Luke* resumes his story with Jesus appearing to be baptized by John—eighteen years later. This eighteen-year period is known as "the hidden years," because there is nothing known about them.

2. "The Hidden Years"

But if the Gospels yield little on "the hidden years" the apocryphal narratives attempt to tell all about them. They begin with the parents of his mother, the well-born Joachim and his beautiful wife, Anna. And a number of stories dwell on the trials and sorrows they endured before their daughter, Mary, was born to them in Nazareth.

There is no hint anywhere in the Gospels as to what Mary looked like. But the apocryphal works give a detailed description of her as a young girl:

Mary was of medium stature, and her body was graceful and well proportioned. She was delicate in appearance and her skin the color of ripening wheat. Her face was oval but not pointed; her hair was golden and not plaited; her eyes were large, bluish in color, and sparkling; her eyebrows were arched and darker in color than the hair of her head; her nose was rather long; and her lips were fresh and full of loveliness in speech. Her hands were long and her fingers tapered. And her appearance was always so beautiful and glorious that scarcely anyone could look into the brightness of her face.

This was the vessel; lovelier still was the content.

None was more learned than Mary in the Law and the Prophets; none was more humble; none more melodious in singing; none more steadfast in the work of the temple. Daily she advanced in the perfection of knowledge and skill. She spoke little, and only that which was necessary; and then with becoming modesty, without embarrassment, and without pride. She was never seen angry, or ever heard to speak ill of anyone. And she was always careful in her speech, lest she offend one of her companions.

And all who knew her, adored her.

The lore proceeds unhurriedly giving every event in Mary's life, accounting for all that remained unexplained in the Gospels; and makes clear how Mary came to be the ward of the aged carpenter, Joseph; and how she was watched over and cared for by five virgins, named Rebekah, Sephora, Susanna, Abigea and Calah.

While the Gospel of *Matthew* devotes less than two chapters to the Story of Jesus from his birth to his baptism at the Jordan; and the Gospel of *Luke* sketches in a single chapter the life of Jesus from his birth to the period of his ministry, in the uncanonical gospels, the lineage, infancy, boyhood and early manhood of Jesus became an inexhaustible source for myriads of stories. And they relate the marvels and miracles attending every event in his life, beginning with the birth of his mother, to the time he meets John the Baptist. Some of these stories arose very early, like those found in *The Provengelium of James* and in *The Gospel of Thomas*. Others are of recent origin, as in *The Aquarian Gospel,* which appeared at the beginning of the twentieth century in the United States.

Many are the fascinating speculations on where Jesus spent "the hidden years." One account is given in a strange book called *The Unknown Life of Jesus Christ,* by Nicolas Notovich, which claims that high in the Himalayan mountains, in the Convent of Himis, there is a scroll written in Pali, which relates:

When Issa [Jesus] was thirteen years old, the age at which an Israelite is expected to marry, the modest house of his industrious parents became a meeting-place of the rich and illustrious, who were anxious to have as a son-in-law the young Issa, who was already celebrated for the edifying discourses he made in the name of the All-Powerful. Then Issa secretly absented himself from his father's house; left Jerusalem, and, in a train of merchants, journeyed toward the Sindh, with the object of perfecting himself in the knowledge of the word of God and the study of the laws of the great Buddhas.

Another claim was made about a century ago when a certain Baron von Rabenau came into possession of Coptic papyri in Egypt, which were presumably translations from the Greek, written in A.D. 83. These papyri, which became known as *The Letter of Benan,* attempt an ingenious explanation of "the hidden years." The account relates that at the age of twelve, Jesus went to Egypt, where he befriended a medical student named Benan, son of a priest of Memphis. Jesus resolved to study the art of healing, and soon astounded his teachers by his skill and wondrous cures.

And there are many other such legendary explanations.

"The hidden years" remain a constant lure. For quite recently Charles Potter, in his appraisal of *The Great Religious Leaders,* comments: "The discovery of the Quamram Scrolls and the comparison of them with the teachings of Jesus lead us to infer he may have spent part, at least, of the 'Silent Years' in Quamram."

3. The Ministry of Jesus

While there is no doubt of the historicity of Jesus, little is known of his childhood and youth. Although he grew up with the Greek and Roman cultures at his doorstep, they did not concern him. He knew no languages other than his mother tongue. He traveled no further than could be covered in two or three days on foot. And at the age of thirty he had created no ripple of excitement among his people. Then, like so many of his contemporaries, he went down to the River Jordan to be baptized by John the Baptist; and it was after this event that his ministry began.

The length of his ministry has never been determined with exactness. But at the most it lasted three years. As soon as he started to preach he attracted disciples, and with them he went about the countryside, preaching to the people and healing the sick. There were many itinerant preachers and faith healers in his day and in his country. But what Jesus preached was unlike anything preached elsewhere in the land.

He went among the poor and downtrodden, healing the sick and comforting the sorrowful, easing the burden of those who were heavy-laden, and bringing hope into the hearts of the repentant. And when he was reprimanded for associating with sinners, he replied: "Those who are well have no need of the physician, but those who are sick. I came not to call the righteous, but sinners to repentance."

Early in his ministry, when a multitude gathered to hear him, he preached to them what has since become known as *The Sermon on the Mount*. This sermon contains the essentials of his teachings.

4. The Sermon on the Mount

And he lifted up his eyes on his disciples and said:

"Blessed are the poor in spirit, for theirs is the kingdom of God.

"Blessed are they who mourn, for they will be comforted.

"Blessed are the meek, for they will inherit the earth.

"Blessed are they who hunger and thirst after righteousness, for they will be filled.

"Blessed are the merciful, for they will obtain mercy.

"Blessed are the pure in heart, for they will see God.

"Blessed are the peacemakers, for they will be called the children of God.

"Blessed are they who are persecuted for righteousness' sake, for theirs is the kingdom of heaven.

"Blessed are you when men revile you and persecute you and say all manner of evil against you falsely for my sake. Rejoice and be exceedingly glad, for great is your reward in heaven, for thus they persecuted the prophets who were before you.

"You are the light of the world. A city set on a hill cannot be hid. Nor do men light a lamp and put it under a bushel, but on a stand, and it gives light to all who are in the house. Let your light so shine before men that they may see your good works and glorify your Father who is in heaven.

"Think not that I have come to destroy the law or the prophets; I have not come to destroy but to fulfill.

"For verily I say to you: Till heaven and earth pass away, not one jot or one dot will pass from the law till all be fulfilled.

"Whoever therefore breaks the least of these commandments, and teaches men so, he will be called the least in the kingdom of heaven; but whoever fulfills and teaches them, he will be called great in the kingdom of heaven.

"You have heard that it was said to those of old, 'You shall not kill, and whoever kills will be in danger of the Judgment.' But I say to you that whoever is angry with his brother will be in danger of the judgment; and whoever says to his brother, 'You fool,' will be in danger of a fiery hell.

"Therefore, if you bring your gift to the altar and there remember that your brother has anything against you, leave your gift before the altar and go; first be reconciled with your brother, and then come and offer your gift at the altar.

"You have heard that it was said, 'You shall not commit adultery.' But I say to you that whoever looks on a woman to lust after her has already committed adultery with her in his heart.

"And if your right eye offend you, pluck it out and cast if from you; for it is better for you that one of your members should perish than that your whole body should be cast into hell.

"Again, you have heard that it was said to those of old, 'You shall not swear falsely, but shall perform to the Lord your oaths.' But I say to you: Do not swear at all; neither by heaven, for it is God's throne, nor by the earth, for it is His footstool; neither by Jerusalem, for it is the city of the great King; neither shall you swear by your head, because you cannot make one hair white or black. But let your 'Yea' be 'Yea' and your 'Nay' be 'Nay,' for whatever is more than this comes of evil.

"You have heard that it was said, 'An eye for an eye and a tooth for a tooth.' But I say to you: Do not resist evil; but whoever smites you on your right cheek, turn to him the left cheek also. And if any man wishes to sue you and take away your coat, let him have your cloak also. And whoever compels you to go a mile, go with him two.

"Give to him who asks from you, and from him who would borrow of you do not turn away. Treat others as you wish them to treat you.

"You have heard that it was said, 'You shall love your neighbor and hate your enemy.' But I say to you who hear: Love your enemies, do good to those who hate you, bless those who curse you, and pray for those who abuse you, that you may be the children of your Father who is in heaven; for he makes his sun rise on the evil and on the good, and sends rain on the unjust as well as on the just.

"For if you love those who love you, what reward should you have? For sinners also love those who love them. And if you do good to those who do good to you, what reward should you have? For sinners also do the same.

"And if you lend to those from whom you hope to borrow, what reward should you have? For sinners also lend to sinners, to receive as much again.

"But I say to you, love your enemies, and do good, and lend, expecting nothing in return; and your reward will be great, and you will be the children of the Highest, for he is kind to the unthankful and to the evil. Therefore be merciful, as your Father also is merciful.

"Take heed that you do not give alms before men, to be seen by them, for then you will have no reward from your Father who is in heaven. Therefore when you give alms, do not sound a trumpet before you as the hypocrites do, that they may have glory from men. Verily I say to you, their reward is glory from men. But when you give alms, do not let your left hand know what your right hand does, that your alms may be in secret; and your Father who sees in secret himself will reward you openly.

"And when you pray, you shall not be like the hypocrites; for they love to pray standing in the synagogues and at the corners of the streets, that they may be seen by men. Verily I say to you, their reward is only that of being seen of men. But you, when you pray, enter into your room; and when you have shut your door, pray to your Father in secret; and your Father who sees in secret will reward you openly.

"And when you pray, use not vain repetitions as the heathen do, for they think that they will be heard for their multitude of words. Be not therefore like them, for your Father knows what you need before you ask him.

"Moreover, when you fast, be not like the hypocrites, of a sad countenance, for they disfigure their faces that they may appear to men to fast. But you, when you fast, anoint your head and wash your face, that you may not appear to men to fast, but to your Father who is in secret; and your Father who sees in secret will reward you openly.

"Lay not up for yourselves treasures upon earth, where moth and rust corrupt and where thieves break through and steal; but lay up for yourselves treasures in heaven, where neither moth nor rust corrupt, and where thieves do not break through and steal; for where your treasure is, there also will be your heart.

"The light of the body is the eye; if therefore your eye be sound, your whole body will be full of light. But if your eye is not sound, your whole body will be full of darkness. If therefore the light that is in you is darkness, how great is that darkness!

"Therefore I say to you: Do not worry about your life, what you shall eat or what you shall drink; nor yet for your body, what you shall put on. Is not the life more than food, and the body than raiment? Behold the birds of the air, for they do not sow, neither do they reap, nor gather into barns; yet your heavenly Father feeds them. Are you not much better than they?

"Which of you by worrying can add one cubit to his stature? And why do you worry about clothes? Consider the lilies of the field, how they grow; they toil not, neither do they spin; yet I say to you that even Solomon in all his glory was not arrayed like one of these. Wherefore, if God so clothe the grass of the field, which today is green and tomorrow is cast into the oven, will he not much more clothe you, O you of little faith?

"Therefore do not worry, saying, 'What shall we eat?' or 'What shall we drink?' or 'With what shall we be clothed?' For all these things do the Gentiles seek, and your heavenly Father knows that you need all these things. But seek first the kingdom of God and his righteousness, and all these things will be added to you. Do not worry about the morrow, for the morrow will take care of itself. Sufficient to the day is the evil thereof.

"Judge not, and you will not be judged; condemn not, and you will not be condemned; forgive, and you will be forgiven. Give, and it will be given to you; good measure, pressed down, shaken together and running over, men will give to you. For with the same measure that you give, it will be measured to you in return. Therefore, whatever you wish men to do to you, do the same also to them, for this is the law and the prophets.

"And why do you note the speck that is in your brother's eye, but do not perceive the beam that is in your own eye? You hypocrite, take out first the beam from your own eye, and then you will see clearly to take the speck out of your brother's eye.

"Do not give what is holy to dogs; neither cast your pearls before swine, lest they trample them under their feet and turn and rend you.

"Beware of false prophets who come to you in sheep's clothing, but inwardly are like ravenous wolves. You will know them by their fruits. Do men gather grapes from thorns or figs from thistles? Even so every good tree yields good fruit, but a bad tree yields evil fruit. Out of the good measure of his heart a good man brings forth that which is good; and so also out of the evil treasure of his heart an evil man brings forth that which is evil; for out of the abundance of the heart the mouth speaks.

"Not everyone who says to me 'Lord, Lord' will enter into the kingdom of God, but he who does the will of my Father who is in heaven. Therefore whoever hears these sayings of mine and does them, I will liken to a wise man, who built his house upon a rock; and the rain descended, and the floods came, and the winds blew and beat upon that house, but it fell not, for it was founded upon a rock. And everyone who hears these sayings of mine and does not do them is like a foolish man, who built his house upon the sand; and the rain descended, and the floods came, and the winds blew and beat upon that house; and it fell, and great was its fall."

5. The Parables of Jesus

In his sermons, Jesus often used parables to underscore his teachings. And the sermons of his brief ministry are studded with them. Some of the parables, like "The Pearl of Great Price," are given in a single sentence; others, like "The Prodigal Son," have the development of a brief story.

The following is a selection from the parables:

● THE PARABLE OF THE SOWER

Behold, a sower went out to sow. And when he sowed some seed fell by the wayside, and the birds came and devoured them. Some fell upon stony places, where they had little earth; and at once they sprang up, but when the sun came up they were scorched, and because they had no root they withered away. Some fell among thorns, and the thorns sprang up, and choked them. But others fell into good ground and brought forth fruit, some a hundredfold, some sixty-fold, some thirtyfold.

● THE TARES AND THE WHEAT

The kingdom of God is like a man who sowed good seed in his field, but while men slept, his enemy came and sowed weeds among the wheat and went his way. But when the blade sprang up, then appeared the weeds also. So the slaves of the householder came and said to him, "Sir, did you not sow good seeds in your field? From where then come the weeds?" He answered them, "An enemy has done this." The slaves said to him, "Do you wish us then to go and gather them up?" But he said, "No, lest while you gather up the weeds, you root up also the wheat along with them. Let both grow together until the harvest; and in the time of harvest I will say to the reapers, 'Gather first the weeds and bind them in bundles to burn, then gather the wheat into my barn.' "

● THE PARABLE OF THE MUSTARD SEED

To what may we liken the kingdom of God and with what may we compare it? It is like a grain of mustard seed which, when sown on the earth, is less than all the seeds that are on earth, but when it is sown, it comes up and becomes greater than all herbs and shoots out great branches, so that the birds of the air may lodge under its shade.

● THE PARABLE OF THE DRAGNET

The kingdom of God is like a net that was cast into the sea and gathered fish of every kind. When it was full they drew it to shore, and sat down and gathered the good fish into vessels, but cast the bad away. So shall it be at the end of the age: the angels will come forth and separate the wicked from the just and cast them into the furnace of fire. And there will be wailing and gnashing of teeth.

● THE UNJUST STEWARD

The kingdom of heaven is likened to a certain king who wished to settle accounts with his servants. When he had be-gun to reckon, one was brought to him who owed him ten thousand talents. But as he could not pay, his lord commanded him to be sold, with his wife and children and all that he had, and payment to be made. The servant fell down and worshiped him, saying, "Lord, have patience with me and I will pay you all." Then the lord of that servant was moved with compassion, and released him and forgave him the debt.

But the same servant went out and found one of his fellow servants, who owed him a hundred *denarii;* and he laid hands on him and took him by the throat, saying, "Pay me what you owe." His fellow servant fell down at his feet and begged him, "Have patience with me and I will pay you all." But he would not, and cast him into prison until he should pay the debt.

So when his fellow servants saw what had been done, they came and told the king. Then the king summoned him and said to him, "O you wicked servant, I forgave you all that debt because you pleaded with me. Should you not also have had compassion on your fellow servant, even as I had pity on you?" And the king was angry and delivered him to the jailers until he should pay all his debt.

* THE PRODIGAL SON

A certain man had two sons. And the younger of them said to his father, "Father, give me the portion of goods that falls to me." And he divided his goods between them. Not many days afterwards the younger son gathered all he had and went on a journey to a far country and there wasted his substance in riotous living. And when all he had was spent, there arose a mighty famine in that land, and he began to be in want. He went and joined himself to a citizen of that country, who sent him into his fields to feed swine.

And he would fain have filled himself with the husks that the swine ate, but no one gave anything to him. But when he realized his situation, he said to himself, "How many of my father's hired servants have bread enough and to spare, while I perish with hunger! I will arise and go to my father and will say to him, 'Father, I have sinned against heaven and before you and am no longer worthy to be called your son; treat me as one of your hired servants.' "

And he arose, and went to his father. When he was still a great way off, his father saw him and had compassion, and ran and fell on his neck and kissed him. The son said to him, "Father, I have sinned against heaven and in your sight and am no longer worthy to be called your son." But the father said to the servants, "Bring out the best robe and put it on him. And put a ring on his hand and shoes on his feet. Then bring the fatted calf and kill it, and let us eat and be merry.

For this my son was dead and is alive again; he was lost and is found." And they began to be merry.

Now the elder son was in the field, and as he returned to the house, he heard music and dancing. He called one of the servants and asked what these things meant. The servant said, "Your brother has come home, and your father has killed the fatted calf, because he has received him safe and sound."

Then he became angry and would not go in. His father came out and besought him. But he said to his father, "Lo, these many years I have served you, nor transgressed at any time your commandment. Yet you never gave me a kid that I might make merry with my friends. But as soon as this your son came who has devoured your living with harlots, you have killed for him the fatted calf." And the father said to him, "Son, you are always with me, and all that I have is yours. It was fitting that we should make merry and be glad. For your brother was dead and is alive, he was lost and is found."

● THE GOOD SAMARITAN

"A certain man went down from Jerusalem to Jericho and fell among thieves, who stripped him of his raiment and wounded him and departed, leaving him half dead. By chance there came down that way a priest; and when the priest saw him, he passed by on the other side. And likewise a Levite, when he came to the place and saw him, passed by on the other side. But a certain Samaritan, as he journeyed, came to where the wounded man was; and when the Samaritan saw him, he had compassion on him and went to him and bound up his wounds, pouring on oil and wine; and set him on his own beast, and brought him to an inn and took care of him. On the morrow, when the Samaritan was about to depart, he took out two *denarii* and gave them to the innkeeper and said to him, 'Take care of him. And whatever more you spend, when I come again, I will repay you.' Now which of these three, do you think, was neighbor to him who fell among the thieves?"

And the scribe said, "He who showed mercy on him." Then said Jesus to him, "Go, and do likewise."

● THE PEARL OF GREAT PRICE

The kingdom of God is like a merchant seeking fine pearls, who, when he had found one pearl of great price, went and sold all that he had and bought it.

6. The Agrapha and Logia

Often Jesus used sayings in his sermons. As late as A.D. 1859 a German scholar, Lobegott von Tischendorf, discovered a Greek Bible in the Convent of St. Catherine at the foot of Mount Sinai, which contained a few hitherto unauthenticated sayings. And about two decades later, two British archaeologists, Drs. Grenfell and Hunt, found in Upper Egypt a number of papyri, chiefly in Greek. Among the papyri was a leaf belonging somewhere between A.D. 150 to A.D. 300, on which there were written a group of sayings attributed to Jesus.

The sayings, which supplement his parables and sermons, are called Agrapha (meaning, Unwritten) and Logia (sayings attributed to Jesus, which are not in the Gospels).

I am thou, and thou art I, and where thou art there am I also; and in all things am I sown. And from whencesoever thou gatherest me, in gathering me thou gatherest thyself.

He who seeks will find; and finding, will wonder; and wondering, will reign; and reigning, will rest.

The soul must be made to grow through faith and knowledge.

Kind words are better than ointment, and a sweet saying than the perfume of love.

A cheerful countenance is as the appearance of sweetness.

Love rules willing hearts; fear, the unwilling.

The giver is happier than the receiver.

Never be joyful, except when you have seen your brother in love.

Love covers a multitude of sins.

You see your brother; you see your God.

There are those who stretch the warps and weave nothing.

Blessed is he who also fasts for this, that he might feed the poor.

You have dismissed the living, who were before you, and talk of the dead.

When you fast, pray for those who are about to perish.

A man not tempted is not proved.

Anger destroys even the prudent.

Where there are pains, thither runs the physician.

Excepting for a few saints, men have always thought that they could atone for their crimes with money.

You hear with one ear, but the other you have closed.

If anyone does not work, let not such a one eat; for the Lord our God hates the slothful.

The Heavenly Father desires rather the repentance than the punishment of sinners.

The world shall be built up through grace.

Show yourself a tried money-changer, in that you can distinguish between good and bad coin.

Ask great things, and the small shall be added; ask heavenly things, and the earthly shall be added.

He to whom more is forgiven, loves more.

No one shall be called good who mixes evil with the good, for gall does not mix well with honey.

Men must give an account of every good word that they fail to speak.

If you cannot keep that which is small, who will entrust you with that which is great? For he that is faithful in very little, is also faithful in much.

As you judge, so shall you be judged.

Blessed are they who mourn the destruction of the unbelievers.

Let us resist all iniquity and hold it in hatred.

Beware how you sit with sinners.

Take not the world for your lord; lest it take you for its slave.

One day Jesus and his disciples passed a man who spoke evil of them in a loud voice; but Jesus spoke only good in return. And when his disciples asked him why he spoke good to him who spoke evil, he replied: "Each gives out of his store."

These and other teachings of Jesus, and his being hailed by his followers as the expected Messiah, stirred the ire of the priesthood and awoke the suspicion of the Roman rulers of Judea. And when he and his disciples came to Jerusalem to celebrate the feast of the Passover, as was customary among the Jews, Jesus was arrested and accused of treason before Pontius Pilate, the Roman Procurator in Judea. Jesus refused to defend himself. And he was condemned to be crucified, according to the method of execution commonly practiced by the Romans.

After his crucifixion, his devoted apostles and disciples scattered to all the neighboring countries in which the Jews had found refuge. And there they preached to their exiled brothers the glad tidings of their Lord Jesus, the Messiah.

7. Paul of Tarsus

In spite of the flush of enthusiasm accompanying its early growth, the new sect might have disappeared, as so many other sects had appeared and were soon gone, were it not for a young man (who had not known Jesus) whose help was called upon to destroy it.

The young man's name was Saul. And he came from Tarsus, a city in Cilicia, where there was a large Jewish community. Because Saul was a Roman citizen, he was called by his Romanized name, Paul. And because his father was a rich merchant, he received a good education. It is believed that he first attended the University of Tarsus, where he studied languages and the philosophies of his time. Then he was sent by his father, who wished him to become a Rabbi, to study under the celebrated Rabbi Gamaliel, a grandson of Rabbi Hillel, famous among his people.

Paul, according to an apocryphal description of him, was short, bowlegged, thick-set and hollow-eyed. Yet he was so gifted a speaker that all who heard him forgot his appearance and saw his face as full of grace. He was reared in the strictest tradition of the Jews and aligned himself early with the traditionalists in the Rabbinic interpretation of the Law and the Prophets.

When his studies were completed, Paul returned to Tarsus. But soon afterwards word was sent to him that the leaders of the newly formed sect of Nazarenes were undermining the Holy Law in Judea. And he was asked to return to Jerusalem and help put down the leaders of the dissident group.

Paul went back to Jerusalem. And there he took part in condemning to death a leader of the Nazarenes, named Stephen. After the public stoning of Stephen, the New Testament tells us, "Paul laid waste the church (of the new sect) and entering house after house, he dragged off men and women and committed them to prison."

From Jerusalem, Paul went on to Samaria, where the Nazarenes had a following; and from there he started out for the city of Damascus, where they were gaining many converts. In the Acts of the Apostles, the account is given:

Now as he journeyed he approached Damascus, and suddenly a light from heaven flashed about him. And he fell to the ground and heard a voice saying to him, "Saul, Saul, why do you persecute me?" And he said, "Who are you, Lord?" And he said, "I am Jesus, whom you are persecuting; but rise and enter the city, and you will be told what to do." The men who were traveling with him stood speechless, hearing the voice but seeing no one. Saul arose from the ground; and when his eyes were opened, he could see nothing; so they led him by the hand and brought him into Damascus. And for three days he was without sight, and neither ate nor drank.

After this mystic experience Paul dedicated himself with zeal to the missionary work of the new sect, preaching the Gospel and strengthening its adherents, the Nazarenes, whom he called by the Greek name, Christians: meaning Followers of the Messiah.

He went about preaching from synagogue to synagogue outside Jerusalem, still believing that there was no conflict between the Law and the Gospel. But when he concluded that the Gospel was meant not for Jews only, but for all mankind, he began to minister to all who would listen to him. He also made changes in the tenets of the new sect, and the sect turned into a separate religion, Christianity. Paul continued fervently organizing the new religion, and by the time he died, Christianity had taken root among the Gentiles.

The young religion was bitterly persecuted and many endured martyrdom, until the Emperor of Rome, Constantine, became a convert to the new faith in the year A.D. 312, and issued an edict granting religious liberty throughout the Roman world. The persecutions ended. And from then on Christianity continued to expand and grow.

8. The Multiplication of Sects

From the very beginning violent differences erupted among the apostles and disciples of Christianity. In its formative period some were opposed to the inclusion and conversion of Gentiles unless they first became converted to Judaism and complied with the rite of circumcision, as well as other basic traditions. Later, when the church became a symbol of the mystical body of Christ, Christianity began to divide into strongly antagonistic branches.

The new religion retained much of Judaism, from which it arose, and incorporated the Hebrew Scriptures as part of its sacred books; and when the new religion became dominant in the Roman and Greek worlds, it transformed and blended some aspects of the native religions—which the people did not wish to give up—and absorbed them.

There arose the Greek Catholic Church, the Roman Catholic Church, the Coptic Church, the Armenian Church, the

Nestorian Church, and various orders and divisions within these churches. Much later, when a Roman Catholic monk, Martin Luther, who was professor of philosophy at the University of Wittenberg, Germany, openly proclaimed his opposition to certain practices of his church, a new and major rift occurred, known as the Reformation. And it was not long before the group of reformers, or Protestants, as they came to be known, also differed among themselves on what they wanted to reform and what they wanted to reject altogether.

The number of Protestant sects increased as Christianity grew, until today there are over 250 of them, varying in strength and following. There are Adventists, Anabaptists, Baptists, Calvinists, Congregationalists, Lutherans, Methodists, Presbyterians, and the others (many of them having their own subdivisions) all the way to the Unitarians and Universalists.

A mere listing of the Christian sects and denominations in the three major divisions and an indication, however briefly, on how they arose and wherein they differ, would fill a long book.

9. The Apostles' Creed

The basic doctrines of Christianity are summed up in what is known as the Apostles' Creed, of which there are a number of variations. The earliest form, known as the Old Roman Creed, of the second or third century, was followed by the Nicene Creed, which was adopted about three centuries later. Since then there have been other creeds varying slightly from the original Roman Creed but underscoring the supremacy of one church over another.

1. I believe in God, Father Almighty,
2. and in Christ Jesus, His only-begotten Son, Our Lord,
3. who was born of the Holy Ghost and of Mary, the Virgin,
4. who was crucified under Pontius Pilate and buried;
5. on the third day He rose from the dead,
6. ascended into heaven,
7. and sitteth at the right hand of the Father,
8. from whence He shall come to judge the quick and the dead;
9. and in the Holy Ghost;
10. the Holy Church;
11. the remission of sins;

12. and the resurrection of the dead.

The Elizabethan Thirty-nine Articles are Calvinistic in their theology, and enounce the royal supremacy in the Church of England.

10. What Christianity Believes

However the various divisions and sects may differ in underscoring or verbalizing their creeds, they are all Christian and have in common these basic beliefs:

In God, Creator of things visible and invisible. He is; and He manifests himself in all reality.

That Jesus is the Messiah, the Christ, Son of God (whether symbolically or literally interpreted).

In the Trinity: The Father, the Son, and the Holy Ghost.*

That man is born a sinner and in need of redemption and salvation.

That Jesus Christ came down to earth for the salvation of mankind.

That man has an immortal soul, accountable to God.

That the Bible (both Old and New Testaments) is the accepted guide to follow.

In the historicity of the Gospels.

In baptism as a remission of sin.

In the repentance of sinners.

In the Life Hereafter.

That those who follow Jesus Christ and who repent their sins, will enter the Kingdom of Heaven.

10 ISLAM

Submission to Allah

1. In the Days before Katum

In the land of Arabia the people of long ago, like others before them, made deities of the sun and the stars, and their spirits, and represented them by images, which they wor-

---

* This belief is not held by Unitarians and Universalists, who have a combined following of about 175,000.

shiped. In time other idols were added—one for each of the 360 days of the Arab year.

They revered also the memory of their forefathers, Abraham and Ishmael. And an old Arabian legend gives the story of their progenitor:

A desert chieftain named Abraham * lived in the desert with his two wives, one named Sarah and the other, Hagar. Sarah, the first wife, was childless, but Hagar gave birth to a boy, and he was named Ishmael. Ten years later Sarah, too, gave birth to a son, and he was named Isaac. Then Sarah feared Ishmael would claim to be the heir and receive the first-born's share of his father's inheritance. She pleaded with her husband to have Hagar and her son banished.

Abraham was grieved by Sarah's plea, but he sent Hagar and the boy away into the desert. The mother and child wandered about for a long time in the cruel heat of the day. Then Hagar sat down on a rock and began to weep, for she feared that she and her son would perish from thirst. Ishmael stood beside her and kicked the hot sand underfoot. And at once, from the spot his foot had kicked, the fresh waters of a spring began to gush. (And, according to legend, that spring has been flowing ever since.)

When Abraham heard of the miracle in the desert, he came to Hagar and Ishmael, and named the spring *Zemzem,* or the Spring of Ishmael. Nearby he built a cubic temple, called *Kaaba* (the Cube), and into the eastern corner of this temple he set the Black Stone, which had been handed down to him as an inheritance from Adam. This Black Stone was brought by Adam from the Garden of Eden when he and his wife were banished from it; and wherever the stone may be, toward it the face of every True Believer is turned in prayer.

Near the temple built by Abraham, Hagar and her son remained. When Ishmael grew up, he married and raised a large family. And his offspring multiplied until they became a great nation. Around the temple grew a large city, called Mecca. And the Children of Ishmael took possession of the land as far East as the Persian Gulf, as far North as the Mediterranean Sea, and as far South as the Gulf of Aden.

But Mecca remained their Sacred City. They made pilgrimages to it to kiss the Black Stone; to drink of the sacred and healing waters of the Spring of Ishmael; and to worship at the *Kaaba.*

So the legend runs.

The Children of Ishmael, in addition to these sacred

* "Abraham was not a Jew or a Christian, but he was an upright man, a Moslem, and not an idolater." (*Koran*)

shrines, worshiped the sun, the moon and the stars. And they filled their temples with idols, 360 idols, one for each day in their year; and these also they worshiped. Sacredness was attributed to certain rocks, trees and hills. And the land was dotted with sacred stones, sacred palms, sacred hills, which the people believed could heal or bring good fortune, and to which pilgrimages were made for hundreds of miles over the desert. And since they were divided into many tribes and lived isolated from each other most of the time, each community developed idols and superstitions of their own, which nurtured rivalries and resulted in feuds between the tribes.

Arabs everywhere, however, believed in the holiness of the *Kaaba,* the Spring of Ishmael, and the city in which they were to be found, Mecca.

This faith began to weaken in time. For merchants of the holy city insisted that the Spring of Ishmael belonged to them and began to sell its healing waters to the pilgrims streaming into the city. Doubt grew. And the people turned to gambling, drinking and fortune-telling. The desire to learn what the future may hold has a fascination for us all. Attempts have been made through the ages to solve this mystery. The Arabs' procedure —a favorite among many other people—was through star-gazing; through dissecting birds and mice—another pattern common to other people even though they chose different creatures to dissect; or by drawing lots, which was the simplest of them all.

Drawing lots had one drawback. It could easily lead to gambling, and it did. Gambling spread among the people, and the gambling led to various other undesirable practices. Among the rich and noble, horsemanship was a popular diversion; and the scholarly held poetry contests; but the poor and uneducated, which were the vast majority of the population, found their pleasure in wine, in wife-stealing, and in gambling.

Gambling dens and every vice flourished in Mecca alongside the temples and the Spring of Ishmael. Sorcerers and soothsayers abounded. Stargazers and diviners competed with the sorcerers and necromancers; and the market places teemed with knaves, swindlers and drunkards.

2. The Seal of the Prophet

Into this atmosphere of superstition, idolatry and depravity, in the heart of Mecca and in the full glare of history, a new faith was born. If we know little about the early days of its founder, other than what was written about him by his followers and admirers after his death, it is because no one could foretell when he was young that he was destined to have such an enduring influence, not only over his own people but over a large part of mankind. In fact, not until he was a middle-aged man was there any sign to indicate that he would become one of the few men whose name would become a part of history.

It all began in this way:

In or about A.D. 570, in the city of Mecca, a child was born into an aristocratic family of the Koreish tribe. Later, after his death, legends arose about the many miracles that accompanied his birth. The stars sang in praise of God, and mountains and valleys responded, lauding the newborn child. Temples crumbled in far-off countries. And in distant Persia, in the temples of Zoroaster, the Eternal Fire which had burned steadily for centuries, suddenly went out. The earth quaked with joy, and idols all over the world tumbled down from their pedestals. And everywhere the omens foretold that a great and godly man-child had been born to cleanse the earth of idolatry and corruption.

In the house of the infant's mother there was no rejoicing. For her husband had died a short time after their wedding and she was still mourning him when her child was born. She sent word to her aging father-in-law, Abu Al-Muttalib, who was a leader in Mecca; and he came and took the infant before the altar of the *Kaaba* to be named. Following the traditional custom of the Arabs of that day, he named the child Kutam, Kutam Mohammed, meaning Kutam, the Praised. The name "Kutam" has been forgotten even by multitudes of his followers, and he is known the world over as Mohammed (or, the Praised).

Mohammed was only six when his mother, too, died. He passed into the care of his aging grandfather and, according to legend, the grandfather kept the boy beside him wherever he went. And in their talks together, the old man gradually taught him all he had learned during his seventy years.

At six years of age Mohammed was ready for school. But his grandfather died. And the orphan went to live with his uncle, Abu Talib, a camel trader and guide for caravans crossing the desert. The boy was not sent to school. He worked in the stables helping to care for his uncle's camels. And when he grew a little older, Mohammed accompanied his uncle on long journeys to the well-known market places of the East, assisting Abu Talib with his merchandise-laden camel caravans.

Though Mohammed had not learned to read and write, during those journeys to Yemen, Syria, Abyssinia, Persia and Egypt, he often met Jewish and Christian merchants, and heard from them about the beliefs of Judaism and Christianity. His parched mind absorbed and stored whatever he learned from them. As he grew older he thought more and more about his people, and during the long monotonous desert crossings he began to meditate on how his people could be won away from idolatry.

He left his uncle when he reached the age of twenty and became the caravan guide and steward of a wealthy and attractive widow, named Khadijah. He soon proved himself completely trustworthy and a capable merchant. And he finally married the lovely Khadijah, although she had forty to his twenty-five years. In spite of the difference in age, the marriage was a happy one. Mohammed became a rich and respected merchant of Mecca, and devoted himself for the next fifteen years to his wife's affairs.

3. La Ilaha Illa Allah

Each year, during the hot summer month of Ramadan, Mohammed retreated with his family to a cave in the desert, where he spent his time in meditation.

One day he was sleeping in the cave when he heard a voice commanding him to read.

"I cannot read," he answered.

Again the Voice commanded him to read. Mohammed explained again that he could not. When the command was given a third time, he asked, "What shall I read?" And the Voice answered:

"Read: In the name of Allah, the Beneficent and Merciful. Read: in the Name of Allah who created man of a clot. Read: And your Lord is most Bounteous, And he teaches man by the pen, he teaches man what he knows not."

Upon awakening, Mohammed remembered what the Voice had said as clearly as if the words had been inscribed upon his heart. He came out of the cave. And again he heard the Voice:

"O Mohammed, you are Allah's messenger and I am Gabriel."

This revelation distressed Mohammed. He confided in Khadijah, and his wife tried to calm and reassure him. When the revelations came to him with increasing frequency, she sent for a learned scribe to record the visions, which Mohammed called "The Reading," because the Angel Gabriel commanded him to read.

After some time, when a number of visions had come to Mohammed, and encouraged by his wife's confidence in him, he went out to preach sermons on them. Few, he found, would believe in him. The people of Mecca at first scoffed; but when he began to preach against the belief in many idols, they threatened to persecute him. During three years of preaching he could win only a handful of converts, and these consisted of his wife, other members of his family, his scribe, and relatives.

But Mohammed persisted.

Many more visions came to him, and his faithful scribe, Abu Bekr, recorded them. Whenever and wherever Mohammed could find a circle of listeners, he would give a sermon on each of his visions. Slowly, very slowly, his circle widened and the number of his listeners gradually increased.

Then the steadfast and loyal Khadijah died, after twenty-six years of marriage. And his loss left Mohammed grief-stricken. But he went on, and preached to the growing number of his followers. The Meccans had long since stopped scoffing. They became alarmed when Mohammed began to direct his sermons against the corruption of the merchants and leaders, and they plotted to kill him.

Mohammed learned of the plot in time to escape to Yathrib, a city about two hundred miles away from Mecca. And the night he fled, the night of June 20, A.D. 622, became the most memorable in Islam, the religion founded by Mohammed. It is called the Night of the Flight, *Anno Hegira*. And just as Jews count the years from the Week of Creation, and Christians count the years from the birth of Jesus, so Mohammedans, or rather Moslems (True Believers) as they prefer to be called, count time from the year of the Flight (Anno Hegira, or A.H.).

The name of the city to which Mohammed fled, Yathrib, was changed to Medina al Nabu (the city of the kingdom of the Prophet), and shortened to Medina. And there Mohammed quickly and vigorously organized his followers into an army, which he led to convert the people to his new faith, which he called Islam, meaning the Submission (to God).

Eight years passed from the fateful Night of the Flight before Mohammed returned to his birthplace, Mecca. He had fled at night under cover of darkness, but he returned in broad daylight at the head of an army of thousands of followers. The people in the city ran away when they heard of his coming, in their fear of Mohammed's revenge.

According to legend, Mohammed rode through the empty city directly to the sacred Temple. And without alighting from his camel, he pointed to the first idol he saw, and said:

"Truth is come, and falsehood is fled away!"

And his followers tore the idol down.

Mohammed moved from idol to idol, until every one of the three hundred and sixty idols was smashed. But he would not allow his followers to touch anything else in the Temple which the people considered sacred; nor would he allow them to plunder the abandoned and unguarded goods in the city.

When the people returned and found that Mohammed had only destroyed the idols and was not intent upon plunder and revenge, they accepted his teachings and enrolled in his army of True Believers. Within two years Mohammed had converted to his teachings not only the Meccans, but all the people of Arabia.

And then, at the age of sixty-two, Mohammed died.

4. The Growth of Islam

Upon the death of Mohammed, his faithful scribe and friend, Abu Bekr, became the first Caliph, or Successor. Plans to establish Isalm as a missionary world religion had already been drawn up before the death of its founder; and Caliph Abu Bekr made preparations to carry them out.

He began to collect his Master's speeches and sermons into a book, called the *Koran,* which means "The Reading." And he organized the Faithful into armies which were to go out and subdue those tribes that had revolted against Islam and had returned to the worship of idols.

Several years later the collection and canonization of the *Koran* was completed. And the Holy Wars with neighboring tribes and countries went on.

When the *Koran* was completed it became a powerful instrument which held Islam together and gave it strength. To the Moslem, the True Believer, every word in the *Koran* is the actual Word of God as revealed to Mohammed by the Angel Gabriel, and some Moslems often memorize it from beginning to end. The *Koran* consists of 114 Suras, or divisions, which vary in length. The longest takes up over a tenth of the book, and the shortest have only three verses. Westerners who read it in translation find it confusing, as they find most sacred books of other religions. The *Koran* is written in classical Arabic, the language in which the Angel Gabriel revealed it to the Prophet, and the Faithful believe that is the language it should be read in. The *Koran* as we have it now does not follow the order in which it was revealed to the Prophet. About ninety Suras were revealed to him before the flight from Mecca. The rest came later. After the *Koran* was canonized, all other versions extant were destroyed.

With the *Koran* to weld them together, the armies of True Believers marched out beyond the confines of their own country to convert other peoples to Islam.

Less than a century later, the Green Flag of the Prophet waved victoriously over Syria and Egypt, and had reached Tunis and Algeria. The conquests of Islam continued. Today this religion is followed by peoples of different races in Africa and Asia, and includes groups of Kurds, Caucasians, Mongols and Chinese.

Although no very reliable accounts are obtainable on the numbers of Moslems, it is estimated that there are about three to four hundred million of them in the world today.

5. The Spread of Islam

The wide spread of Islam has puzzled many scholars. They can find nothing in its teachings that cannot be found, and traced to, the teachings of Judaism and Christianity. And certainly in its early stages, it depended upon Holy Wars in which the Sword preceded the Word. However, the Moslem armies in their early period poured into areas where a corrupt priesthood served innumerable idols, and oppressed and confused the people with superstitious beliefs. This may be one of the historical factors in the rapid spread of Islam.

The Moslems themselves attribute their impact to the *Koran*, which addresses itself to the downtrodden, the hopeless and the poor, the ignorant and the outcast, regardless of race or color, or nationality. This approach, based on the idea of the equality of all men before God, had and still has a great appeal, particularly in areas where people are divided into castes, and where some are considered so low in the scale of humans that they are not even permitted to enter a House of Prayer.

Islam also won the hearts of simple people by doing away with intermediaries between God and man. No matter how lowly a man may be, or how ignorant, or how sinful, he needs no other than himself to bring his plea for help or forgiveness before God.

Nor do Moslems need to go to a temple or mosque to communicate with Allah. The first confession of belief of every Moslem is: "God is One and Mohammed is his Prophet." Therefore God is everywhere, and every place on earth is as holy as any other where one may stop to pray; and wherever one prays, that spot is holy ground. Each Moslem carries with him a little prayer rug. When he wishes to pray, he takes off his shoes, spreads out the prayer rug, and kneels down facing Mecca.

Their belief that all men are equal before Allah; that no man needs another to intercede for him before God; that God is everywhere, and every place is holy ground where man communes with his Creator—these simple basic teachings, so the Moslems say, account for Islam's success among various peoples in the world.

The followers of Islam are constantly reminded of their faith and its tenets. Five times each day every Moslem must pray a simple prayer. This prayer, known as *Al-Fatitah,* consists of the opening verses of the *Koran:*

Praise be to Allah, Lord of the Worlds,
The Beneficent, the Merciful,
Master of Judgment Day,
You do we worship and You we beseech for help;
Guide us on the right path,
The path of those whom You have favored,
And not of those upon whom You have brought down Your wrath
And have gone astray.

Then he may recite a prescribed portion of the *Koran*.

On Friday, the Islamic Sabbath, the prayers are more elaborate.

As simple as the Islamic prayers, are the duties of the True Believer. They are called the Five Pillars of the Faith:

1. The duty to recite the creed: There is no God but Allah, and Mohammed is his Prophet. That is the First Pillar.

2. The duty to worship One God and pray to Him five (at least three) times each day. That is the Second Pillar.

3. The duty to practice charity and help the needy. That is the Third Pillar.

4. The duty to fast in the month of Ramadan, when the *Koran* was revealed as a guide to mankind. That is the Fourth Pillar.

5. The duty to make the pilgrimage to Mecca at least once in a lifetime, if possible. That is the Fifth Pillar.

And upon these Five Pillars Islam rests.

These are duties easily explained, easily understood and, with the exception of the pilgrimage, easily carried out.

6. What Islam Believes

1. *One God.* The first belief of Islam is the belief that there is One God, who is the giver of all that is good in man's life. Therefore God must be always in the hearts and minds of men, and True Believers must pray to him five times each day.

2. *Sacred Ground.* All the earth belongs to Allah and therefore wherever one prays is holy ground. That is why every Islamic prayer begins with the *Al-Fatitah,* the opening verses of the *Koran.*

3. *Equality Before God.* No man needs an intercessor before Allah. All men are equal in the eyes of God. He makes no distinction between rich and poor; learned or ignorant; white, black or yellow; rulers of empires, or humble shepherds who care for their flocks.

4. *Life Hereafter.* Man's physical body dies, but his soul lives forever. When the soul is emancipated from the body in death, it goes either to heaven or to hell. (Both are described in great detail in the *Koran.*) Man's conduct when his body is alive determines his fate in the life hereafter.

5. *Drunkenness Prohibited.* Islam considers intoxicating drinks as "the mother of all evil," and drunkenness as a sin.

6. *Truthfulness.* To tell the truth at all times and under all circumstances is a commandment from God: "O you Moslems, stand fast to Justice, when you bear witness, though it is against yourself, or your parents, or your kin, rich or poor. God is nearer to you than any. Therefore follow not passion, lest you swerve from the Truth."

7. *Adultery Forbidden.* "There is nothing which Allah abhors more than adultery," is written in The Sayings of Mohammed. It goes farther and states: "The eye and the tongue can commit adultery."

8. *Charity.* Charity is stressed in the *Koran* and in The Sayings of Mohammed, called *Hadith.* Charity is carried out not only in almsgiving, but in the kindness and concern one human being shows for others. Every act of kindness is charity.

9. *Duty to Animals.* Kindness must be extended even to animals. "There is no beast on earth nor bird that flies, but the same is a creature like unto you, and to God shall they return," is written in the *Koran.* Therefore man must treat dumb animals with kindness and compassion.

10. *Limited Polygamy.* A Moslem is allowed to marry

four wives, provided he can take care of them. Otherwise he may marry only one.

And in the Sixth Sura of the *Koran,* we find the equivalent of a code:

Come, and I will recite to you that which your Lord has commanded you to do:

Ascribe nothing as partner to Allah;

Show kindness to your parents;

Slay not your children for fear of poverty—Allah will provide for them;

Come not near polluted things, open or concealed;

Slay no one, except for the requirements of justice;

Do not approach the property of an orphan to improve it, until he comes of age;

Give full measure and a just balance;

In judgment observe justice, even in the affairs of a kinsman;

Fulfill your covenant with Allah; and

Follow no other paths, lest you depart from Allah's path.

7. Chapters from the Koran

● THE CHAPTER OF THE FORENOON

In the name of the merciful and compassionate God.

By the forenoon!

And the night when it darkens!

Thy Lord has not forsaken thee, nor hated thee! and surely the hereafter is better for thee than the former; and in the end thy Lord will give thee, and thou shalt be well pleased!

Did He not find thee an orphan, and give thee shelter? and find thee erring, and guide thee? and find thee poor with a family, and nourish thee?

But as for the orphan, oppress him not; and as for the beggar, drive him not away; and as for the favor of thy Lord, discourse thereof.

● THE CHAPTER OF UNITY

In the name of the merciful and compassionate God.

Say, "He is God alone!

God the Eternal!

He begets not and is not begotten!

Nor is there like unto Him anyone!"

● THE CHAPTER OF THE NIGHT

In the name of the merciful and compassionate God.
By the night when it veils!
And the day when it is displayed!
And by what created male and female!
Verily, your efforts are diverse!
But as for him who gives alms and fears God,
And believes in the best,
We will send him easily to ease!
But as for him who is niggardly,
And longs for wealth,
And calls the good a lie,
We will send him easily to difficulty!
And his wealth shall not avail him
When he falls down (into hell)!!
Verily, it is for us to guide;
And, verily, ours are the hereafter and the former life!
And I have warned you of a fire that flames!
None shall broil thereon, but the most wretched, who says it is a lie and turns his back.
But the pious shall be kept away from it, he who gives his wealth in alms, and who gives no favor to anyone for the sake of reward, but only craving the face of his Lord most High; in the end he shall be well pleased!

● THE CHAPTER OF THE LAND

In the name of the merciful and compassionate God.
I need not swear by the Lord of this land, and thou a dweller in this land!
Nor by the begetter and what he begets!
We have surely created man in trouble.
Does he think that none can do aught against him?
He says, "I have wasted wealth in plenty"; does he think that no one sees him?
Have we not made for him two eyes and a tongue, and two lips? and guided him in the two highways? but he will not attempt the steep!
And what shall make thee know what the steep is? It is freeing captives, or feeding on the day of famine, an orphan who is akin, or a poor man who lies in the dust; and again (it is) to be of these who believe and encourage each other to patience, and encourage each other to mercy—these are the fellows of the right!

But those who disbelieve in our signs, they are the fellows of the left, for them is fire that closes in!

● THE CHAPTER OF THE SMITING

In the name of the merciful and compassionate God.
The smiting!
What is the smiting?
And what shall make thee know what the smiting is?
The day when men shall be like scattered moths; and the mountains shall be like flocks of carded wool!
And as for him whose balance is heavy, he shall be in a well-pleasing life.
But as for him whose balance is light, his dwelling shall be the pit of hell.
And who shall make thee know what it is?—a burning fire!

● THE CHAPTER OF THE CLEAVING ASUNDER

In the name of the merciful and compassionate God.
When the heaven is cleft asunder,
And when the stars are scattered,
And when the seas gush together,
And when the tombs are turned upside down,
The soul shall know what it has sent on or kept back!
O man! what has seduced thee concerning thy generous Lord, who created thee, and fashioned thee, and gave thee symmetry, and in what form He pleased composed thee?
Nay, but ye call the judgment a lie! but over you are guardians set—noble, writing down! they know what ye do!
Verily, the righteous are in pleasure, and, verily, the wicked are in hell; they shall broil therein upon the judgment day; nor shall they be absent therefrom!
And what shall make thee know what is the judgment day? Again, what shall make thee know what is the judgment day? a day when no soul shall control aught for another; and the bidding on that day belongs to God!

● THE CHAPTER OF THOSE WHO TEAR OUT

In the name of the merciful and compassionate God.
By those who tear out violently!
And by those who gaily release!
And by those who float through the air!
And the preceders who precede!

And those who manage the affair!*

On the day when the quaking quakes which the following one shall succeed! Hearts on that day shall tremble; eyes thereon shall be humbled!

They say, "Shall we be sent back to our old course?— What! when we are rotten bones?" They say, "That then were a losing return!"

But it will only be one scare, and lo! they will be on the surface!

Has the story of Moses come to you? when his Lord addressed him in the holy valley of Tuva, "Go unto Pharaoh, verily, he is outrageous: and say, 'Hast thou a wish to purify thyself, and that I may guide thee to thy Lord, and thou mayest fear?'"

So he showed him the greatest signs; but he called him a liar and rebelled. Then he retreated hastily, and gathered, and proclaimed, and said, "I am your Lord most High!" but God seized him with the punishment of the future life and of the former.

Verily, in that is a lesson to him who fears!

Are ye harder to create or the heaven that he has built? He raised its height and fashioned it; and made its night to cover it, and brought forth its noonday light; and the earth after that he did stretch out. He brings forth from it its water and its pasture.

And the mountains He did firmly set, a provision for you and for your cattle.

And when the great predominant calamity shall come, on the day when man shall remember what he strove after, and hell shall be brought out for him who sees!

And as for him who was outrageous and preferred the life of this world, verily, hell is the resort!

But as for him who feared the station of his Lord, and prohibited his soul from lust, verily, Paradise is the resort!

They shall ask thee about the Hour, for when it is set. Whereby canst thou mention it? Unto thy Lord its period belongs.

Thou art only a warner to him who fears it.

On the day they see it, it will be as though they had only tarried an evening or the noon thereof.

* Opening lines refer to the angel of death and his assistants, who "tear" away the souls of the wicked violently, and gently "release" the souls of the good; and to the angels who "precede" the souls of the righteous to Paradise.

● THE CHAPTER OF THOSE SENT

In the name of the merciful and compassionate God.

By those sent in a series!

And by those who speed swiftly!

And by the dispensers abroad!

And by the separators apart!

And by those who instill the reminder, as an excuse or warning!

Verily, what ye are threatened with shall surely happen!

And when the stars shall be erased!

And when the heavens shall be cleft!

And when the mountains shall be winnowed!

And when the apostles shall have a time appointed for them!

For what day is the appointment made?

For the day of decision! and what shall make thee know what the decision is?

Woe on that day for those who say it is a lie!

Have we not destroyed those of yore, and then followed them up with those of the latter day?

Thus do we with the sinner.

Woe on that day for those who say it is a lie!

Did we not create you from contemptible water, and place it in a sure depository unto a certain decreed term? for we are able and well able too!

Woe on that day for those who say it is a lie!

Have we not made for them the earth to hold the living and the dead? and set thereon firm mountains reared aloft? and given you to drink water in streams?

Woe on that day for those who say it is a lie!

Go off to that which ye did call a lie! Go off to the shadow of three columns, that shall not shade nor avail against the flame! Verily, it throws off sparks like towers—as though they were yellow camels!

Woe on that day for those who say it is a lie!

This is the day when they may not speak—when they are not permitted to excuse themselves!

Woe on that day for those who say it is a lie!

This is the day of decision! We have assembled you with those of yore; if ye have any stratagem, employ it now!

Woe on that day for those who say it is a lie!

Verily, the pious are amid shades and springs and fruit such as they love. "Eat and drink with good digestion for that which ye have done!"

Verily, thus do we reward those who do well.

Woe on that day for those who say it is a lie!

"Eat and enjoy yourselves for a little; verily, ye are sinners!"

Woe on that day for those who say it is a lie!

And when it is said to them bow down, they bow not down.

Woe on that day for those who say it is a lie!

And in what new discourse after it will they believe?

- THE CHAPTER OF THE RESURRECTION

In the name of the merciful and compassionate God.

I need not swear by the resurrection day!

Nor need I swear by the self-accusing soul!

Does man think that we shall not collect his bones? Able are we to arrange his finger tips!

Nay, but man wishes to be wicked henceforward! he asks, When is the resurrection day!

But when the sight shall be dazed, and the moon be eclipsed, and the sun and the moon be together, and man shall say upon that day, "Where is a place to flee to?"—nay, no refuge! and to thy Lord that day is the sure settlement: He will inform man on that day of what he has sent forward or delayed!

Nay, man is an evidence against himself, and even if he thrusts forward his excuses—.

Do not move thy tongue thereby to hasten it. It is for us to collect it and to read it; and when we read it then follow its reading. And again it is for us to explain it.

Nay, indeed, but ye love the transient life, and ye neglect the hereafter!

Faces on that day shall be bright, gazing on their Lord!

And faces on that day shall be dismal!

Thou wilt think that a back-breaking calamity has happened to them!

Nay, but when the (soul) comes up into the throat, and it is said, "Who will charm it back?" and he will think that it is his parting (hour). And leg shall be pressed on leg; unto thy Lord on that day shall the driving be.

For he did not believe and did not pray; but he said it was a lie, and turned his back! Then he went to his people haughtily—woe to thee, and woe to thee! again woe to thee, and woe to thee!

Does man think that he shall be left to himself?

Wasn't he a clot of emitted seed? Then he was congealed

blood, and (God) created him, and fashioned him, and made of him pairs, male and female.

Is not He able to quicken the dead?

8. Sayings from the Koran

O People! Serve Allah who created you and those who went before you. He made the earth as your resting place and the sky as your canopy; and he sends down rain from heaven to bring forth fruit with which to sustain you. As long as you know this, set up no rivals to Allah!

Will you order men to be pious and yourself forget it?

Those who have faith and do good works are the rightful owners of the Garden (of Eden) and will dwell in it.

Allah is in the east and Allah is in the west; wherever you turn, there is Allah's face.

In the alternation of day and night, in the rains from heaven that come to quicken the parched earth, in the shifting winds, and in the clouds pressed into service between heaven and earth, there are signs enough of Allah's rule for people who have understanding.

When misfortune strikes, say, "Verily, we all come from Allah and to Allah we must return."

Allah loves all those who do good.

Allah is with those who patiently endure.

If you give alms publicly, it is well; but it is better to give them secretly. Allah knows what you do.

Wrong not and you will not be wronged.

Pleasant for mankind is the love of women and children, and the joy of gold and silver, and well-bred horses, and cattle, and land. But Allah, with him is the best resort.

Do not pray when you are drunk, until you know what you utter.

Whatever good befalls a man, it is from Allah; whatever ill befalls a man, it is his own doing.

Those who deny Revelation shall not enter Paradise until the camel goes through the eye of a needle.

Every nation has its prophet; every nation has its time.

The Lord said to the bee: "Choose your habitation in the hills and build your hives in the trees; eat of every fruit and walk in the path of the Lord." And the bees out of their body produce honey which is a cure for men. Verily these are signs for men to reflect upon.

If you do good, you do good for your own souls; if you do evil, you do it to yourselves.

No soul shall bear the burden of another.

The wastrel is the devil's brother.

He who is blind in this life will be blind in the Hereafter.

Every soul must taste of death.

He who takes guidance from others than Allah might be likened to the spider building his house; surely the frailest of all houses is the house of the spider.

Were all the trees on earth pens, and the sea with seven more seas to increase it, ink, they would still not suffice for the words of Allah.

Repay evil with good and, lo, he between whom and you there was enmity will become your warm friend.

Can the reward of goodness be aught but goodness?

Wait for us that we may kindle our candle by yours.

Do no favors in order that you may later receive them in return with increase.

Man loves the transitory and neglects the eternal.

As the day declines, man is in a state of loss, save those who have faith and do good works.

11 ZOROASTRIANISM

The Refugee Religion

1. Zend Is Not Zen

Zend should not be confused with *Zen*. The two are only distantly related. Whereas *Zen* goes with Buddhism (as we shall see later), *Zend* goes with *Avesta*.

The *Zend-Avesta* (the Law and the Commentaries) is the name of, or rather part of, the sacred books of a religion that was founded in Persia in the seventh century B.C., and which had almost completely disappeared from the land of its birth by the seventh century A.D. During these fourteen centuries—from about 700 B.C. to about A.D. 700—nearly all the sacred books of all the great religions were created, assembled and canonized. And on practically all of them the religion of the *Zend-Avesta* exerted a great influence, directly or indirectly. The religion was known by many (not quite accurate) names: Mazdeism, Magism, Fire-Worship, Parsiism, Dualism, and Zoroastrianism.

Curiosity and interest in this religion existed in the centuries immediately preceding and immediately following the birth of Christ. Greek philosophers and historians in particular speculated about it and wrote dissertations on its basic beliefs. Herodotus and Plutarch among the Greek historians, and Aristotle and Plato among the Greek philosophers, showed an interest in any teachings that bore the name "Zarathustra," which came to be used as an equivalent of "wisdom." At one time the names of Zarathustra and Plato were treated as belonging to the same school of philosophy.

Then the interest died down. Throughout the Middle Ages almost nothing was known about this faith excepting the name of its founder, Zarathustra, whom the Greeks called Zoroaster. And Zoroaster was conceived of as a Magus, a member of the ancient Akkadian priestly tribe of Magi, and a master of secret sciences related to Fire-Worship.

Toward the beginning of the eighteenth century a remnant of worshipers who followed this religion, called Parsees (Persians), who had found refuge in India, aroused interest and their beliefs were studied. But the scant scriptures remaining to them were preserved neither in Sanskrit nor in Prakrit, nor in any of the other languages of their adopted land; and European scholars had difficulty in deciphering them. Early in the eighteenth century the English obtained from the Persians in India a copy of these scriptures, called the *Zend-Avesta,* and, since they could not translate it, they hung the book up by a chain on a wall of the Bodleian Library at Oxford University, as a curiosity to be shown to visitors.

About a quarter of a century later, a young student at the School for Oriental Languages in Paris, Anquetil Duperron, happened to see a few facsimile pages of the curious book in the Bodleian Library, and he made up his mind to break its seal of mystery. He went to India to study with the Parsees. And ten years later, after many adventures and hardships, Duperron returned to Paris and triumphantly deposited with the French Royal Library a complete translation of the *Zend-Avesta.* The seal of mystery had at last been broken.

2. When Iran Was Called Persia

Close to the landlocked Caspian Sea, west of Afghanistan, there lived many centuries ago a hardy and industrious people in a land called Persia, which is now known as Iran. The country was rugged and the climate trying. The Iranians, who were farmers and shepherds, had to work extremely hard to survive. In their struggle for existence they enlisted the help of many Nature-gods: the Rain-god to water the fields; the Sun-god to ripen the crops; the Fertility-god to increase the flocks; and a host of other gods. Like early Nature-worshipers in other lands, they created idols to represent the forces of nature in concrete and familiar images. And they worshiped these idols.

While many of the Nature-gods were good and beneficent, there were also vindictive and destructive gods to contend with: the god of floods and the god of drought, both equally harmful; the god of windstorms that dried out the newly-planted fields, carrying away topsoil and seed, and leaving desolation; and the dreaded gods of disease and pestilence that brought suffering and death. All these gods, the people believed, had to be propitiated.

Since the pressing need to tend the fields and herd the sheep and cattle kept the people hard at work most of the time, the task of worshiping the good gods and conciliating the malevolent spirits was left to a group of men considered especially learned and wise in such matters. These men they called priests.

Temples were built where the idols of the good and evil gods were kept. And on the appropriate occasions the priests chanted hymns and offered up sacrifices accompanied by the proper prayers. The good gods seemed pleased with prayers and hymns, but the evil gods were not so easily influenced. The priests, who sought for ways in which to propitiate the gods of destruction, began to claim that they had found a method by which they could influence the gods. The method was called Magic, and the priests who could practice this Magic were called Magi.

Belief in the mysterious power of the Magi spread among the simple hard-working farmers, shepherds and cattlemen of Iran. And belief in magic and sorcery swept the land.

3. The Magician's Nightmare

In the year 660 B.C., according to legend, the Chief Magician of Iran, named Durasan, dreamed the chilling dream that a child had been born who would grow up to destroy idol-worship, banish sorcery, and uproot magic. Through the aid of black magic, Durasan quickly discovered that this child had been born to wealthy parents of the Spitama clan in the city of Azarbijan; and that he had been named Zarathustra.

Durasan and a retinue of his magicians set out to find the child and destroy him. But to their dismay all their plots were frustrated. When they brought Zarathustra to the Temple and placed him on the blazing fire of the altar, the child played about happily in the flames as if he were in the waters of a lukewarm bath; when the infant was placed in the path of a herd of cattle, the first cow that came near stood over the child to protect him until the entire herd had passed, and Zarathustra remained unhurt; and when Durasan and his men abandoned the child in a den of wolves, the hungry wolves could not come near to harm him. These and many other legends were told about how the plots of the Chief Magician of Iran were thwarted.

Zarathustra grew up unharmed by the machinations against him. And when he was old enough, his parents sent him to learn the art of healing. Upon completing his studies, Zarathustra went out to minister to the poor and the sick among his people. As he made his daily rounds among the afflicted, Zarathustra meditated on health and disease, joy and sorrow, life and death, light and darkness, good and evil. He wondered where evil came from and how it could be banished.

One day he came to his wife, Havovee, and told her that he had decided to go up to the top of Mount Sabalan to live as a hermit, so that he could seek in solitude for answers to questions that gave him no peace. And he took leave of his wife and children.

Zarathustra went up to the mountain top, and there he lived in isolation. Months passed. But Zarathustra's long meditations left him no wiser. He could find neither clue nor key to understanding the sufferings that were the lot of man. He was about to abandon his search and return to his family, when suddenly, in a flash of enlightenment, he remembered something he had known from childhood, and which he now recognized as the key he had been seeking: "From good must come good; and from evil must come evil."

The good cannot create evil; and evil cannot, through magic and prayer, create good. This, thought Zarathustra, is because the world was created by two forces: one is the God of Good (*Ahura Mazda* or *Ormuzd*), and the other is the God of Evil (*Angra Mainyu* or *Ahriman*). This concept of the world is called *Dualism.*

Zarathustra, however, did not believe in eternal Dualism. He believed that the God of Good, who had created the world with purifying fire, cleansing water, fruitful earth and sweet smelling air, is at war with the God of Evil, creator of sickness and pestilence, pain and death. If men do good and ally themselves with *Ahura Mazda,* together they will triumph over *Angra Mainyu,* and then only the

God of Good will rule the world. *But the God of Good needs man to help him conquer evil.*

Zarathustra remained in his mountain retreat for some time. There he had many revelations: he saw *Ahura Mazda* face to face; and he learned from *Ahura Mazda* how the world was created, and how on a Day of Judgment, Good will banish Evil. Then Spitama Zarathustra was ready to go down to the people to preach to them the religion of *Mazda,* which would lead them from darkness to light, from suffering to joy, from evil to good.

What had been foretold to Durasan in his troubled dream was about to come true.

4. The Conversion of King Vishtaspa

But the foretold downfall of magic and sorcery did not come quickly.

What appeared to Zarathustra as crystal clear and undeniably true, the people could not and would not accept. They were accustomed to their idols, they were comfortable with them and accepted them without questioning. Zarathustra's Gods of Good and Evil seemed strange and difficult to understand. Not even the members of Zarathustra's own family were willing to give up the gods they had always believed in for the new teachings. For ten years Zarathustra patiently tried to gain a following but without success.

In desperation, he travelled to Balkh, a city in Bactria, where King Vishtaspa lived. At the gate of the Royal Palace he asked the guard to announce him to the king.

"And who are you?" asked the guard.

"Go, and tell King Vishtaspa that I, Spitama Zarathustra, have come to preach the True Religion, the religion of the Holy One, *Ahura Mazda,* and to turn him and his court away from the worship of idols to the worship of the Beneficent One."

And as a sign that he was the True Prophet of *Ahura Mazda,* Zarathustra stretched out his right hand. In his palm a ball of fire burned brightly, yet the hand was not burned.

The guard went at once to inform King Vishtaspa. And the King said: "Go, bring him in!"

Zarathustra appeared before the King and began to explain his teachings. For three days he remained at court, debating with the King's priests and magicians, answering their questions, and explaining that *Ahura Mazda* created everything that is good in the world, while *Angra Mainyu* counter-created all that is evil in the world. For every good thing created by *Ahura Mazda,* its evil opposite was counter-created by *Angra Mainyu.* When the Good God created light, the Evil One created darkness. When the Good God created life, the Evil One created death. When the Good God created health, the Evil One created illness. Everything Good has its opposite in Evil.

"Will this be eternally so?" the King asked.

"No," answered Zarathustra. "There will come a day, the Judgment Day, when *Ahura Mazda* will conquer and banish *Angra Mainyu."*

"And when will that be?" asked the King's High Priest.

"When man allies himself with *Ahura Mazda* and helps him to banish all that is evil, all that is darkness, and all that is death."

Then he outlined man's part as ally of the God of Good. When he had finished, the Chief Magician asked how Zarathustra could prove these things he had spoken of were true. Zarathustra replied that he had spoken directly with *Ahura Mazda,* who had revealed himself on Mount Sabalan.

Then Zarathustra spoke of himself in the third person, as he related:

Ahura Mazda spake unto Spitama Zarathustra, saying: "I have made every land dear to its people, even though it had no charms whatever in it. Had I not made every land dear to its people, even if it had no charms whatever in it, then the whole living world would have invaded the *Airuana Vaego.*

"The first of the good lands and countries which I, *Ahura Mazda,* created was the *Airuana Vaego,* by the Vanguhi Daitya. Thereupon came *Angra Mainyu,* who is all death, and he counter-created the serpent in the river and Winter, a work of the Devas. There are ten winter months there, two summer months; and those are cold for the waters, cold for the earth, cold for the trees. Winters fall there, the worst of all plagues.

"The second of the good lands and countries which I, *Ahura Mazda,* created, was the plain which the Sughdhas inhabit. Thereupon came *Angra Mainyu,* who is all death,

and he counter-created the locust, which brings death unto
cattle and plants.

"The third of the good lands and countries which I,
Ahura Mazda, created, was strong, holy Mouru. Thereupon
came *Angra Mainyu,* who is all death, and he counter-
created plunder and sin."

Zarathustra went on to describe a dozen other countries
created by *Ahura Mazda.* And he ended with quoting *Ahura
Mazda* as saying:

"There are still other lands and countries, beautiful and
deep, longing and asking for the good and bright."

Upon completing his revelation of the Creation of the
Material World, Zarathustra recounted:

Zarathustra asked *Ahura Mazda:* "O *Ahura Mazda,* most
beneficent Spirit, Maker of the material world, thou Holy
One! Who was the first mortal, before myself, Zarathustra,
with whom thou, *Ahura Mazda,* didst converse, whom thou
didst teach the Religion of *Ahura?*"
Ahura Mazda answered: "The fair Yima, the good shepherd, O holy Zarathustra! he was the first mortal, before
thee, Zarathustra, with whom I, *Ahura Mazda,* did converse, whom I taught the Religion of Ahura, the Religion
of Zarathustra. And the fair Yima, O Zarathustra, replied
unto me, saying: 'I was not born, I was not taught to be
the preacher and the bearer of thy Religion.' Then I, *Ahura
Mazda,* said thus unto him, O Zarathustra, 'Since thou dost
not consent to be the preacher and the bearer of my Religion,
then make thou my world increase, make my world grow:
consent thou to nourish, to rule, and to watch over my
world.' And the fair Yima replied unto me, O Zarathustra,
saying: 'Yes! I will make thy world increase, I will make
thy world grow. Yes! I will nourish, and rule, and watch
over thy world.' "

Zarathustra went on to tell of the revelation he had
received about the places on earth where man is most
happy. He had said to *Ahura Mazda:*

"O Maker of the material world, thou Holy One! Which
is the first place where the Earth feels most happy?"
Ahura Mazda answered: "It is the place whereon one of
the faithful steps forward, O Spitama Zarathustra!"

"O Maker of the material world, thou Holy One! Which is the second place where the Earth feels most happy?"

Ahura Mazda answered: "It is the place whereon one of the faithful erects a house with a priest within, with cattle, with a wife, with children, and good herds within; and wherein afterwards the cattle continue to thrive, virtue to thrive, fodder to thrive, the dog to thrive, the wife to thrive, the child to thrive, the fire to thrive, and every blessing of life to thrive."

"A Maker of the material world, thou Holy One! Which is the third place where the Earth feels most happy?"

Ahura Mazda answered: "It is the place where one of the faithful sows most corn, grass, and fruit, O Spitama Zarathustra! where he waters ground that is dry, or drains ground that is too wet."

"O Maker of the material world, thou Holy One! Which is the fourth place where the Earth feels most happy?"

Ahura Mazda answered: "It is the place where there is most increase of flocks and herds."

Zarathustra recited to the court all his other revelations, dwelling on Purity and Impurity, Cleanliness and Uncleanliness.

And he said:

With these words the holy *Ahura Mazda* rejoiced the holy Zarathustra: "Purity is for man, next to life, the greatest good; that purity, O Zarathustra, that is in the Religion of *Mazda* for him who cleanses his own self with good thoughts, words, and deeds."

When the King had heard all Zarathustra's revelations, he called in the Royal Scribes and ordered them to write down on parchment all that Zarathustra had related. And he called the book *Zend-Avesta*. Then he sent out a royal decree which made the teachings of Zarathustra the state religion for all Iranians.

5. A Religion in Exile

For about three centuries the religion of the *Zend-Avesta* thrived in the land of its birth; and the fame of its founder reached to the far corners of the then civilized world. The name Spitama Zarathustra was honored by religious leaders and held in high esteem among philosophers. The Greek philosopher Aristotle wrote about the teachings of Zarathustra (in Greek, Zoroaster) and equated his name with wisdom.

Ironically enough the same Aristotle who extolled the wisdom of Zoroaster was the tutor of Prince Alexander, son of King Philip II of Macedonia. Alexander succeeded his father at the age of twenty and, almost as soon as he was crowned king, went into battle to put down uprisings in Thrace and Thebes. In these he was victorious. But he did not stop fighting. Victory followed victory, until all of Asia Minor was under Alexander's command. Then he marched on Syria, on Babylon and on the Persian Empire. And when he conquered Iran, he ordered the sacred books of the land burned and the native religion replaced by the Greek religion.

And so it came about that a pupil of Aristotle, the great admirer of the teachings of Zoroaster, caused the destruction of the *Zend-Avesta*.

In time the Iranians regained their freedom, and from fragments of the *Zend-Avesta* which they remembered, or had succeeded in secretly preserving, they reconstructed part of it.

Around this period Mohammed had established Islam in Arabia, and his successors had gone out to conquer the world in the name of Allah. By the middle of the seventh century A.D. the Moslems conquered Iran, destroyed the remaining sacred books, and those who refused to submit to Allah were killed. Many Iranians escaped to India, where they found refuge and the freedom to worship as they wished. In India they are called Parsees (Persians) and permitted to practice their religion unhampered. Though their numbers are few, their tenacity to their faith is great. No one attempted to convert them forcibly to another religion; nor did they attempt to convert others. There are only about 140,000 Zoroastrians in the world today, mostly in India.

They are known for their veneration of Fire, Water, and Earth, which they consider sacred, and which must not be polluted. This veneration has given rise to a unique burial practice among them. Since the earth is sacred and cannot be polluted by burying in it a human being or an animal, and since fire, too, is sacred and the dead cannot be cremated lest the fire be polluted, and since water also is sacred, the Parsees build high towers, called Towers of Silence, where they leave their dead to vultures and birds of prey.

The Zoroastrians have severely simple rituals and dignified prayers that embody their basic religious beliefs.

A religion native to India, Jainism, is summed up in one

word: *Ahimsa* (Reverence for Life). Zoroastrianism, a religion in exile in India, is summed up in three words: *Humata, Hakhata, Hvarshta*. Freely translated they mean: The thought well thought, the word well spoken, and the deed well done.

The good deed begins with the good thought. An evil deed is a sin. But so also is an evil speech and an evil thought. The law cannot punish a man for what he thinks. But it is in a man's thoughts that *Angra Mainyu* plots his evil deeds. Therefore, say the Zoroastrians, man must forever examine his heart and mind to keep out evil.

6. What Zoroastrianism Believes

Zoroastrianism believes that the world was created with both good and evil: the good coming from *Ahura Mazda,* and the evil from *Angra Mainyu.*

Man was created by *Ahura Mazda,* but he was given the free will to choose between good and evil.

If man allies himself with *Ahura Mazda, Angra Mainyu* will eventually be conquered. On that day, the Day of Judgment, a happy life will begin for all mankind.

To ally himself with *Ahura Mazda,* man must cleanse his heart and mind of all evil.

Truth is the first virtue.

Charity to all in need is the virtue that comes next.

Man must discipline himself by good thoughts, good words, good deeds (*Humata, Hakhata,* and *Hvarshta*). What is the thought well thought? It is the thought the holy man thinks and which he holds holy before all other things.

What is the word well spoken? It is the word conceived in reason.

What is the deed well done? It is the deed which received the praise of all who regard righteousness above all.

The man who has a wife is far above him who lives in continence; he who has children is far above him who is childless.

A man may pray to *Ahura Mazda* to make him better, to make him happier, but not for evil to befall an enemy.

Because *Ahura Mazda* created fire, water and earth, they must not be polluted, and burial by cremation, by throwing the body into the water, or by burial in the ground is forbidden.

When a man dies, his soul crosses a narrow bridge over hell. The good man crosses over safely to the bright realm of *Ahura Mazda;* the reprobate tumbles down from the bridge into the dark realm of *Angra Mainyu.*

At the end of time there will appear a savior, a Sayoshant, to revive all the dead, to reward the good and to punish the evil-doers. And then *Ahura Mazda* will reign eternally.

Though there are not many Zoroastrians today and their numbers are diminishing, their religion has influenced several of the great religions of the world. And while the ideal of *Ahimsa* is unattainable in a world where the living thrive on the living, the Zoroastrian ideal of "the thought well thought; the word well spoken; and the deed well done" is one that all people can strive for.

7. Three Zoroastrian Prayers

● TO THE EARTH AND THE SACRED WATERS

And now we worship this earth which bears us, together with Thy wives, O *Ahura Mazda!* yea, those Thy wives do we worship which are so desired for their sanctity. We sacrifice to their zealous wishes, and their capabilities, their inquiries, and their wise acts of pious reverence, and with these their blessedness, their full vigor and good portions, their good fame and ample wealth.

O ye waters! now we worship you, you that are showered down, and you that stand in pools and vats, and you that bear forth our loaded vessels, ye female *Ahuras* of *Ahura,* you that serve us in helpful ways, well forded and fullflowing, and effective for the bathings, we will seek you and for both worlds! Therefore did *Ahura Mazda* give you names, O ye beneficent ones! when He who made the good bestowed you. And by these names we worship you, and by them we would ingratiate ourselves with you, and with them would we bow before you, and direct our prayers to you with free confessions of our debt.

O waters, ye who are productive, and ye maternal ones, ye with heat that suckles the frail and needy before birth, ye waters that have once been rulers of us all, we will now address you as the best, and the most bountiful; those are yours, those good objects of our offerings, ye long of arm to reach our sickness, or misfortune, ye mothers of our life!

● PRAYER FOR HELPERS

And now in these Thy dispensations, O *Ahura Mazda!,* do Thou wisely act for us, and with abundance with Thy bounty and Thy tenderness as touching us; and grant that reward which Thou has appointed to our souls, O *Ahura Mazda!* Of this do Thou Thyself bestow upon us for this world and the spiritual; and now as part thereof do Thou grant that we may attain to fellowship with Thee, and Thy Righteousness for all duration.

And do Thou grant us, O *Ahura!* men who are righteous, and both lovers and producers of the Right as well. And give us trained beasts for the pastures, broken in for riding, and for bearing, that they may be in helpful companionship with us, and as a source of long enduring vigor, and a means of rejoicing grace to us for this. So let there be a kinsman lord for us, with the laborers of the village, and so likewise let there be the clients. And by the help of those may we arise.

So may we be to You, O *Ahura Mazda!*, holy and true, and with free giving of our gifts.

● A PRAYER FOR SANCTITY AND ITS BENEFITS

I pray with benedictions for a benefit, and for the good, even for the entire creation of the holy and the clean; I beseech for them the generation which is now alive, for that which is just coming into life, and for that which shall be hereafter.

And I pray for that sanctity which leads to prosperity, and which has long afforded shelter, which goes on hand in hand with it, which joins it in its walk, and of itself becoming its close companion as it delivers forth its precepts, bearing every form of healing virtue which comes to us in waters, appertains to cattle, or is found in plants, and overwhelming all the harmful malice of the Devas, and their servants who might harm this dwelling and its lord, bringing good gifts, and better blessings, given very early, and later gifts, leading to successes, and for a long time giving shelter.

And so the greatest, and the best, and most beautiful benefits of sanctity fall likewise to our lot for the sacrifice, homage, propitiation, and the praise of the Bountiful Immortals, for the bringing prosperity to this abode, and for the prosperity of the entire creation of the holy, and the clean, and as for this, so for the opposition of the entire evil creation.

And I pray for this as I praise through Righteousness, I who am beneficent, those who are likewise of a better mind.

12 ZEN BUDDHISM

Riddles with a Purpose

1. Zen—the Enigma

Among the many religions of the world, and their sub-divisions into sects, some large in number of adherents, and some small, some very old, and some newly evolved, Zen is the most difficult to describe. Everyone, however authoritative and learned, who attempts to define and describe Zen Buddhism to non-Buddhists, begins with an apology and the assurance that the subject is like quicksilver in impatient hands.

The difficulty in describing Zen has an analogy to the story about the villager who returned home from his voyage to an exotic island and attempted to describe one of its fruit, called maypop. Since none of his neighbors had ever seen or even heard of a maypop, he was at a loss as how to begin. At last he said: "Well, you know what an apple is like?"

"Yes," they answered.

"And you know what a pear is like?"

"Yes," came the collective reply.

"And, of course, you know what a peach is like?"

"Yes, yes," they answered impatiently.

"And you know what an apricot is like?"

"Of course, of course."

Then he paused, thought for a while, shook his head and said: "Well, a maypop is unlike any of them."

So, too, in any comparison of Zen Buddhism to other religions, it can only be said that it "is unlike any of them."

In the introduction to *The Essentials of Zen Buddhism* by Daisets Teitaro Suzuki, the eminent Japanese interpreter of Zen to the West, there is this assertion: "Of the current impact of Zen on the West it might perhaps be said that never before have so many evinced such interest in anything so little understood."

"Zen," writes Christmas Humphreys, President of the Buddhist Society in London, "is a subject extremely easy to misunderstand." And he might have added, "extremely difficult to understand."

174

The distinguished philosopher, Dr. Abraham Kaplan, early in his lecture on Zen (as recorded in his book, *The New World of Philosophy*) recounts the legend of a monk who approached a Zen Master with the request for enlightenment about the meaning of Zen. The Master replies: "Tell it to me without words, and I will reply in kind."

A little earlier in his lecture, Dr. Kaplan remarked: "You may complain that if Zen doesn't talk, it can't teach; and Zen will counter, Whoever said that it *is* a teaching? It is *we* who come to Zen in the expectation of being taught; but what we have to learn is precisely to get rid of such expectations."

How, then, is one to learn anything about Zen? How did Zen arise? What are its basic beliefs? If Zen cannot be learned, how can it be attained? What are the disciplines of Zen? What are its objectives?

2. Zen: Seed, Plant and Flower

There exists a great interest in the West about Zen, particularly since World War II. Yet there seems to be a general haziness about the origin of Zen, what it believes, and the disciplines of Zen. The fault is not entirely with the interested-but-uninitiated. The fault lies also with Zen as a deliberately inscrutable teaching, made even more enigmatic by its interpreters, who spend many years writing innumerable books to explain what they insist is utterly inexplicable. Their explanations are frequently interrupted to warn the reader that, in the words of Lao-tze, "they who tell do not know; they who know do not tell."

Many people think of Zen as a Japanese development, manifest in their *Noh* plays, in their flower arrangements, in their dances, in their tea ceremonies, in their art, in their archery. And if they think so, they are within the area of the truth. Some think of Zen as a Chinese interpretation of the Buddhist concept of the state of enlightenment, or of being "awakened," transported and adjusted to Japanese culture. That, too, is within the area of the truth. And then there are some who think that Zen Buddhism goes back to the days of the Buddha in India, when he began to expound Zen, wordlessly.

According to legend, when the Buddha was growing old he convened his disciples for an important discourse. And when they gathered and sat down silently, reverently waiting to hear their aging Master speak, the Buddha arose, came forward on the flower-decked platform, looked over his audience of disciples and monks, then bent down and picked up a flower which he raised to the level of his eyes. Then, without uttering a word, he returned to his seat. His followers looked at each other in bewilderment, not understanding the meaning of his silence. Only the venerable Mahakasyapa serenely smiled at the Master. And the Master smiled back at him and wordlessly bequeathed to him the spiritual meaning of his wordless sermon.

And that, according to legend, was the moment when Zen was born.

Nearly a thousand years passed from the legendary encounter of the Buddha and the venerable Mahakasyapa until Zen, transmitted from generation to generation, reached Bodhi-Dharma, who introduced it to China. And still another century passed before a Chinese philosopher and theologian, Hui-neng, who died in A.D. 713, established Zen as a sect of Buddhism.

In China, the mystic experience of the Buddha's "enlightenment" was influenced by the teachings of Lao-tze. While the seed of Zen came from India, it grew in China and was transformed by Taoism. But it did not reach full flowering until it came, with Chinese Buddhism, to Japan. In Japan, Zen was crystallized into a system, although its adherents insisted that it could not be taught, and argued that there could be no dependence on explanations, on sermonizing or on any formal creed or ritual.

The name "Zen" is Japanese. It derives from the Chinese *Cha'an-na*, which is a corruption from the Buddhist *Dhyana*, meaning Meditation.

Since Zen was adopted and adapted in Japan, it has gone through a number of transformations. For historical reasons, and because of its presumable nihilistic implications, Zen became popular with the intellectual classes in Japan, and its following increased to nearly five million toward the end of the Second World War. And from Japan, Zen was introduced to the West.

3. The Importance of Feeling

Zen teaches the dependence upon oneself rather than upon the search outside oneself for answers to questions and for wisdom. Where the questions come from, Zen maintains, there the answers are to be found. Zen therefore encourages the search *into* rather than *outside* oneself for enlightenment. If the question is properly "felt," the answer is instantly received. The "feeling" is important, rather than the understanding that can be verbalized. Zen depends upon intuition and not upon intellectualization. That is why, Zennists claim, Zen is so difficult to grasp.

To comprehend Zen one must first discipline and restrain the mind through meditation and introspection, without the use of logical thinking, avoiding the pitfalls of verbalization. The ultimate aim is to obtain an entirely new view of all experience. And the key word is *Satori* (enlightenment). This is the experience the Buddha sought in lonely and quiet meditation, and this is the mystic "enlightenment" that every person can find in Zen.

The enlightenment of the Buddha has a distinct difference. The Buddha sought and found a new insight into the reality of things which, to him, meant emancipation from the sorrows of reincarnation. In Buddhist literature there is Buddha's "Song of Awakening," which celebrates his discovery of the door to *Nirvana.*

> Long have I wandered, long!
> Bound by the chain of life,
> Through many births;
>> Seeking thus long in vain
>> Whence comes this life in man, his
>>> conciousness, his pain!
>
> And hard to bear is birth,
> When pain and death but lead to birth again,
> Found! It is found!
>> O Cause of Individuality!
>> No longer shalt thou make a house for me.
>
> Broken are all thy beams,
> Thy ridge-pole shattered!
>> Into *Nirvana* now my mind has passed.
>> The end of cravings has been reached at last!

The enlightenment of Zen, *Satori,* is related to but is not the same as the Buddha's. *Satori* is not concerned with emancipation from the wheel of existence, but rather with gaining new insight into existence, and a new intuitive approach to Being.

This insight cannot be taught or communicated. Each man must find and experience it for himself. And while *Satori* cannot be taught, without attaining *Satori* no one can enter into the truth of Zen. "*Satori* is the *raison d'être* of Zen," Subzuki tells us, "without which Zen is not Zen."

However, there are techniques or disciplines that can help to orient the one who seeks *Satori,* techniques that retrain the mind and attitudes to logical-illogical thinking; to the realization that words are poor and often defective substitutes for facts; that the experience of true reality is possible through facts and not through verbal symbols.

Judaism asserts that the world rests on one pillar, and its name is Justice. Zen also rests on one pillar, and its name is *Satori*.

4. The Mondo and the Koan

The disciplines and the techniques used by Zen in developing the disciple's receptivity to the experience of *Satori* are called *mondo* and *koan*.

The mondo is a question-and-answer method between the Zen Master and the disciple. To the uninitiated it is an opaque dialogue between teacher and disciple, that often seems presented in nonsense-riddles. The *koan* is a statement which the student must fathom by himself. Suzuki asserts that the *koan* is neither a riddle nor a witty remark. "It has a most definite objective, the arousing of doubt and pushing it to its furthest limits."

Here are a few examples of *mondo* and *koan,* of which there are hundreds in Zen:

"Last night a wooden horse neighed and a stone man cut capers."

"Lo, a cloud of dust is rising from the ocean, and the roaring of the waves is heard over the land."

"It is pouring now. How would you stop it?"

"When both hands are clapped a sound is produced: listen to the sound of one hand."

"If you have heard the sound of one hand, can you make me hear it too?"

A Zen Master was asked by a monk: "What is Buddha?" And he replied: "The cat is climbing up the post."

When the monk confessed that he could not understand the Master, the latter said: "You go and ask the post."

Question: "In what way do my hands resemble the Buddha's hands?"

Answer: "Playing the lute in the moonlight."

Question: "In what way do my feet resemble the feet of a donkey?"

Answer: "When the heron stands in snow, its color is not the same."

Suzuki tells of a disciple who asked a Zen Master: "With what frame of mind should one discipline oneself in the truth?"

And the Master answered: "There is no mind to be framed, nor is there any truth in which to be disciplined."

"If there is no mind to be framed and no truth in which to be disciplined, why do you have a daily gathering of monks who are studying Zen and disciplining themselves in the truth?"

The Master replied: "I have not an inch of space to spare, and where could I have a gathering of monks? I have no tongue, and how would it be possible for me to advise others to come to me?"

The questioner then examined: "How can you tell me a lie like that to my face?"

The Master said: "When I have no tongue to advise others, is it possible for me to tell a lie?"

The disciple then said despairingly: "I cannot follow your reasoning."

"Neither do I understand myself," concluded the Zen Master.

5. Zen and Other Faiths

Zen anticipates with a disclaimer all assertions that it is mystical, deliberately paradoxical, and esoteric. Zennists contend that it is not a philosophy or a religion in the Western sense; it neither affirms nor denies the existence of God. It is neither monotheistic nor pantheistic. It has no sacred books. It does not teach or preach any doctrine or set of doctrines. It is not negative or nihilistic.

Zen is a faith of creative experience. It attempts to liberate the mind from the slavery of words and the constriction of logic. Intuition is stressed. And its method of banishing doubt is to push doubt to its extreme.

Zen is not competitive, and does not proselytize. Men of all faiths can attempt to explore it without giving up their own religious beliefs. And through Zen they may explore themselves and, perhaps, find a more intuitive experience in their own beliefs.

A New Image of Reality

As our knowledge of reality widens, and our understanding grows keener of the interdependence of the world, our need increases for faith, for the belief that life has purpose.

The vision of man and our planet as the center of the universe has been shattered. Yesterday, allegorically speaking, the world we lived in was neatly visualized as a huge flat, uneven disc, planted securely in the center of a limited and vaulted space, surrounded by the sun, the moon, and the stars. The earth, when explored on foot, or on the back of a donkey, seemed frighteningly immense in every direction, and as unfriendly as it was vast. And the heavens were comfortably near so that, before "the bridge to heaven" broke down, men could visit those in the heavens, and those in heaven could visit the earth.

Today our knowledge of the universe and its inhabitants has undergone a tremendous change, and our vision of reality has been transformed.

During the period when men lived in sharply separated cultures, they tended to become ethnocentric, that is, each regarded his own culture as superior, desirable, moral and worthy; and considered all other cultures as inferior, ridiculous, immoral and unworthy. This was particularly true of attitudes toward religion. Each saw his own religion as the only true, revealed and moral faith, while all others were deluded and false.

We can no longer remain parochial and ethnocentric. For when we examine the basic beliefs of the most dissimilar people, we discover to our amazement how much alike they are in certain basic respects. As Max Müller told us, "There never was a false god, nor was there really ever a false religion, unless you call a child a false man." In the credos of the living religions we find the important beliefs all affirm a reverence for life; all accept the responsibility for each other's welfare. While differences exist, the similarities are many.

We have entered now into a new dimension of human relationships, and have an unparalleled awareness about ourselves. The most distant parts of the earth are nearer to each other, by jet, than is Jerusalem to Nazareth, on foot.

In the era of atomic power and space exploration, all humanity becomes united. And men are seeking, and may yet discover, a fresh, untired and unifying approach in their faith that life has purpose. An understanding of the beliefs of other peoples is a positive step in this search for a new dimension.

Statistical Table on the
Great Religions

When we try to obtain recent and reliable statistics of the number of adherents of each of the great religions in the world today, we are confronted with an abundance of facts and figures that are, unfortunately, more confusing than informing. This is particularly true of the Oriental religions where a believer may belong to two or more faiths (and is often counted more than once), and where recent and reliable figures are either lacking or are based on some earlier statistics that are now completely out-of-date. In our rapidly changing times, the sources are at best just proximate estimates. The reader who seeks up-to-date and reliable figures is advised to consult current year books (like the World Almanac), the latest supplement of the Encyclopaedia Britannica, the most recent additions to the Encyclopedia of Ethics and Religion; and similar available sources.

Here, in round figures, are the approximate number of adherents of the religions treated in this book as obtained from 1962–3 sources:

Hinduism	336,000,000
Buddhism	153,000,000
Jainism	1,500,000
Confucianism	300,000,000
Taoism	30,000,000
Shinto	50,000,000
Judaism	12,500,000
Christianity	905,000,000
Islam	435,000,000
Zoroastrianism	140,000
Zen Buddhism	5,500,000

The adherents of a number of primitive religions; religions that have originated comparatively recently; and those who claim that they belong to no religion at all add up to about one-half a billion people.

Acknowledgments and Bibliography

History does not repeat itself. However, historians do repeat each other. All history, in whatever field, is a compilation of facts as recorded by former historians, who obtained them from others—all the way back to presumable eye-witnesses. Rarely is history written by those who experienced it. A soldier in a battle is not qualified to write a history of the war in which he is participating. He can only write about his personal and limited experience. When he begins to describe the war, or even a single battle, he must depend upon facts assembled by others. This is true also of the histories of religions. The writer of religious history must depend upon the records of others who may themselves be remote from first-hand factual material. He must depend principally upon those gifted scholars who have assembled with a maximum degree of authenticity the basic documents of each religion.

Anyone working in the field of comparative religion owes a great debt to those dedicated Orientalists of the last century who translated the voluminous Sacred Books of the East, which are the foundations of the world's religions. In this book, the author is particularly indebted to Max Müller, Ralph T. Griffith, James Legge, Sir Edwin Arnold, Herman Jacobi, William Jennings, Jr., Herbert A. Giles and Rhys-Davies.

I am very grateful to Little, Brown & Co., for their permission to quote from *The Bible for Family Reading* and acknowledge with gratitude the permission of Dodd, Mead & Co., to use material from *The Wisdom of the Living Religions*. I am also indebted to the Julian Press, for permission to use Gandhi's letter, from *Reincarnation Anthology*, edited by Joseph Head and S. L. Cranston; and to Rider & Co., England, and to Grove Press (the future American publisher of *Introduction to Zen Buddhism*) for permission to quote from D. T. Suzuki's *Introduction to Zen Buddhism*.

The following list of books is available in most public

libraries. In the field of religion the bibliography is so vast that even if restricted to a selection of books in English, written within the twentieth century, the problem is baffling. The brief list chosen here is merely a start for the layman who may be eager to explore the subject, or certain aspects of the subject, further. And most of these books contain additional bibliographies to guide the reader.

An Introduction to the Study of Comparative Religion, by Frank Ryron Jevons; Macmillan Co., 1920. A transcription of a series of lectures, with emphasis on primitive religions.

The Eleven Religions and Their Proverbial Lore, by Selwyn Gurney Champion; E. P. Dutton & Co., 1945. Another good introduction to comparative religion from the folklore point of view.

How the Great Religions Began, by Joseph Gaer; Dodd, Mead & Co., 1954. The world's living religions presented concisely in terms of the lives, beliefs, and teachings of their founders.

The Great Religious Leaders, by Charles Francis Potter; Simon & Schuster, 1958. A revised edition of an earlier book by the same author, presenting in twenty compact essays the biographies and achievements of a number of religious leaders— from Akhnaton and Moses to Joseph Smith and Mary Baker Eddy.

Had You Been Born in Another Faith, by Marcus Bach; Prentice-Hall, 1961. An original and refreshing presentation of the beliefs and rituals of the living religions, personalizing what your experiences would have been if you had been born into each of the religions of the world.

An Historian's Approach to Religion, by Arnold Joseph Toynbee; Oxford University Press, 1956. An historical appraisal of religion, with which one may agree or disagree, but which offers profitable insights.

The Scriptures of Mankind, edited by Charles Samuel Braden; Macmillan Co., 1952. Excellent collection of selections from the world's sacred books. This book is particularly useful because of the instructive general introduction and the annotated bibliography on each of the religions treated.

The Religions of Mankind, by Edmund Davidson Soper; Abingdon-Cokesbury, 1921. A good general introduction to the entire topic of comparative religion.

Hinduism, by L. D. Barrett; Open Court Publishing Co. (no date of publication given). This brief essay in almost outline form gives the progression in the development of Hinduism from the Vedic Age to the sects of the nineteenth century.

Indian Thought and Its Development, by Albert Schweitzer; Holt, 1936. Contains an excellent introduction to the teachings of Jainism.

Muhammad and Christ, by Moulvi Muhammad Ali; Ahmadia Anjuman-i-Ishaat-i-Islam; Lahore, India, 1921. A valuable book for anyone interested in knowing how the devout Muslims regard the New Testament, in general, and Jesus as he appears in the Gospel. Simply if devoutly presented.

The Teachings of the Compassionate Buddha, edited by E. A. Burtt; New American Library, New York, 1955. An excellent introduction to a very complex topic about which there still exists too little knowledge in the Western world. It contains also a version of "The Dhammapada."

Three Religions of China, by William Edward Soothill; Oxford University Press. Confucianism, Taoism and Buddhism; and how they are regarded in the life of China.

The Story of Confucius, Brian Brown; David McKay, Philadelphia, 1927. A biography of Confucius and a discussion of his ethics; illustrated with many of his best-known sayings which are necessary to an understanding of Confucianism.

The Wisdom of Confucius, Lin Yutang; Modern Library, New York, 1938. This is as good an introduction to Confucius and his teachings as can be found between the covers of a single volume.

The Old Fellow, Herryman Maurer; John Day Co., New York, 1943. A lively and humorous story of Lao-tze, the founder of Taoism. Reads like a novel, but is authentic and scholarly.

Modern Japan and Shinto Nationalism, D. C. Holton; University of Chicago Press, Chicago, 1943. A brief but lucid discussion of Shintoism as a State Religion by a notable authority on the topic and the author of a number of books on Japan and its native religion.

Everyman's Talmud, A. Cohen; E. P. Dutton & Co., New York, 1949. A comprehensive summary of the basic teachings of the Talmud prepared for the lay reader; with a good introduction explaining the historical background of the Talmud and its formation.

Sayings of the Fathers, translated by Joseph H. Hertz; Behrman House, New York, 1945. The late Chief Rabbi of the British Empire presents here in parallel columns the Hebrew and the English text of the *Sayings of the Fathers,* and annotates them with an excellent running commentary.

The Lore of the Old Testament, Joseph Gaer; Little, Brown & Co., Boston, 1951. A collection of extra-canonical stories arranged in sequence to present the characters and events that appear in the Hebrew Scriptures.

Jesus of Nazareth, by Joseph Klausner, translated from the Hebrew into English by Herbert Danby; Macmillan Co., New York, 1925. A great scholarly work, beautifully written, which gives the reader a clear insight into the life of Jesus in terms of the world conditions, in general, at that time, and of the political and economic conditions, in particular, in Palestine. Analyzes the teachings of Jesus and gives the clearest account of the trial and Crucifixion to be found anywhere. As rich in understanding as in scholarship.

The Parables of the Synoptic Gospels, B. T. D. Smith; Cambridge University Press, London, 1937. A good book on the historical background of the parables.

The Lore of the New Testament, Joseph Gaer; Little, Brown & Co., Boston, 1952. A biography of Jesus as it appears in folk imagination; with the lore of the apostles.

Christian Faith and Man's Religion, Mark C. Ebersole, editor; Thomas Y. Crowell Co., 1961. A collection of essays by Karl Barth, Eric Fromm, Reinhold Niebuhr, etc., which give glimpses of the modern approach to faith in general and to Christianity in particular.

Mohammedanism: An Historical Survey, H. A. R. Gibb; Oxford University Press, 1949. Available in a paper-bound edition (Mentor) in 1955. This book gives a bird's-eye view of Mohammedanism from its inception to the present day; and is appended by a bibliography of seventy-seven books for the reader enticed to explore the topic more thoroughly.

The Sayings of Mohammed, Allama Sir Abdulah Al-Manum Al-Suhrwady; The Wisdom of the East series; John Murray, London, 1941. A fairly large collection of Sayings from accepted Hadith sources.

The Dawn and Twilight of Zoroastrianism, by R. C. Zachner; G. P. Putnam's Sons, New York, 1961. A very lucid contemporary history of this religion by a distinguished Oxford don; with an excellent annotated bibliography.

The Ethical Religion of Zoroaster, Miles Meander Dawson; Macmillan Co., New York, 1931. A biography of Zoroaster, with an analysis of his ethics; contains also a comparison of Zoroaster's sayings with those found in Judaism and Christianity.

A History of Zen Buddhism, by Heinrich Dumoulin, S.J.; Pantheon Books. A comprehensive exploration of this very opaque but rewarding subject, written by a Catholic priest.

The Essentials of Zen Buddhism, by D. T. Suzuki, with an introduction by Bernard Phillips; E. P. Dutton & Co., 1962. A comprehensive one-volume introduction to Zen Buddhism, including an orderly sampling of Suzuki's works.

Zen Buddhism, by D. T. Suzuki; Doubleday Anchor Books, 1962. An excellent selection from the writings of D. T. Suzuki, edited by Wm. Barrett.

Meeting with Japan, by Fosco Maraini; Viking Press, 1960. This volume, which presents a multi-faceted view of the people, culture and tradition of modern Japan, obliquely delineates the influence of Shintoism, Buddhism, Taoism and Zen Buddhism on the lives of the Japanese people today.

Index

Abigea, 130
Abraham, 102-104, 105, 106, 118, 146
Abu Al-Muttalib, 148
Abu Bekr, 150, 151
Abu Talib, 148
Abyssinia, 148
Adam, 118
Adventist, 144
Adventures of Rama, 32
Afghanistan, 163
Africa, 152
Agamas, 57
Agrapha and Logia, 140-141
Ahimsa, 57, 59, 171
Ahriman, 165
Ahura Mazda, 165, 166, 167, 168, 169, 171, 172, 173
Allah, 149, 152, 170
Alexander, 170
Alexander, Major General G. G., 78
Algeria, 152
Amaterasu-omi-Kami, 93, 95, 101
Anabaptist, 144
Ancestor-worship, 105
Analects, Book of, 69
Angas, 57
Angi, 30
Angra Mainyu, 165, 166, 167, 168, 171
Animism, 105
Anna, 130
Anno Hegira, 130
Anthropocentric, 22
Anthropomorphous, 105
Aquarian Gospel, 131
Aristotle, 163, 170
Arjuna, 32, 33
Asia, 152
Azarbijan, 164

Babylon, 111, 170
Bactria, 166
Balkh, 166
Baptist, John the; *see* John the Baptist
Baptists, 144
Benares College, 30
Benares, Sermon at; *see* Sermon at Benares

Bhagavad-Gita, 25, 28, 32-35, 36
Birth-Stories, 41, 49
Black Stone, The, 146
B'nai B'rith, 103
Bodhi-Dharma, 176
Bodisat, 41
Bodleian Library, 163
Book of Analects, 69, 71
Book of Annals, 66, 76
Book of Ceremonies, 66
Book of Changes, 65
Book of Good Counsel, 36
Book of Odes, 66
Bo Tree, 43
Brahma, 35
  day of, 23, 25
  night of, 23
Brahman, 30, 35
Brahmanas, 31, 36
Brahmin, 26, 39
Bridge to Heaven, 93
Buddha, 81, 176, 177
  story of, 40-43
Buddhism, Chinese, 176
Buddhist Scriptures, 45
Burma, 43

Calah, 130
Calvinists, 144
Canaan, 105
Caspian Sea, 163
Caste system, 26-27, 35, 55, 56
Cuneciaus, 132
Ceylon, 43
Chaldees, 102, 103
Charity, 47, 59, 110-111, 154
Children of Ishmael, 146
China, 43
Chinese Classics, 76
Ch'iu K'ung; *see* Confuscius
Chou, Province of, 77
Christian Scriptures, 128-129
Christianity, 62, 152
Chuang-tze, 81
Ch'un Ch'in; (Autumn and Spring), 67
Church, Armenian, 144
  Coptic, 144
  of England, 145
  Greek Catholic, 144
  Nestorian, 144

187

MENTOR Religious Classics

☐ **THE MEANING OF THE GLORIOUS KORAN: AN EX-PLANATORY TRANSLATION by Mohammed Marmaduke Pickthall.** The complete sacred book of Mohammedanism. (#MW1195—$1.50)

☐ **THE TEACHINGS OF THE COMPASSIONATE BUDDHA edited with commentary by E. A. Burtt.** The best translations of the writings of the great Oriental religion of Buddhism. (#MY1222—$1.25)

☐ **THE SONG OF GOD: BHAGAVAD-GITA translated by Swami Prabhavananda and Christopher Isherwood.** The timeless epic of Hindu faith. Introduction by Aldous Huxley. (#MQ1003—95¢)

☐ **THE UPANISHADS: BREATH OF THE ETERNAL translated by Swami Prabhavananda and Frederick Manchester.** Concerned with the knowledge of God and the highest aspects of religious truths, these ancient Hindu scriptures are presented in a readable translation. (#MQ921—95¢)

☐ **THE LIVING TALMUD: THE WISDOM OF THE FATHERS AND ITS CLASSICAL COMMENTARIES, selected and translated by Judah Goldin.** A new translation, with an illuminating essay on the place of the Talmud in Jewish life and religion. (#MQ1024—95¢)

☐ **THE SAYINGS OF CONFUCIUS: A NEW TRANSLATION by James R. Ware.** The sayings of the greatest wise man of ancient China, teaching the ageless virtue of civilized men. (#MT1082—75¢)

THE NEW AMERICAN LIBRARY, INC.,
P.O. Box 999, Bergenfield, New Jersey 07621

Please send me the MENTOR BOOKS I have checked above. I am enclosing $_____(check or money order—no currency or C.O.D.'s). Please include the list price plus 25¢ a copy to cover handling and mailing costs. (Prices and numbers are subject to change without notice.)

Name_____

Address_____

City_____State_____Zip Code_____
Allow at least 3 weeks for delivery